Law, Social Movements and the Politics of the Commons

This book reinterprets the notion of the commons by tracing how it has been mobilised in the aftermath of economic crisis.

In a period of widespread activism against the privatisation of resources and services implemented through austerity policies, the reconceptualisation of property as a non-absolute and non-individualistic institution has attracted a great deal of attention. Drawing on the case of the Italian South, and in the wake of economic crisis, this book offers a critical analysis of the struggle for the commons. More specifically, as it details how discourses, legal tools and policies based on disciplinary ideas of the commons are deployed in the neoliberal restructuring of societies, the book considers how conflicting ideas of the commons express different, and often clashing visions, of urban space. In this regard, moreover, it shows how law plays a central, albeit ambivalent, role in the struggle for the commons: as both a governmental technique to regulate urban space and its residents and as an emancipatory tactic to advance non-proprietary visions of ownership.

This book will be of interest to scholars in socio-legal studies, property law, legal sociology and politics, as well as others with more general interests in the critical potential of contemporary social movements.

Veronica Pecile is an Affiliated Researcher at Lucernaiuris – Institute for Interdisciplinary Legal Studies at the University of Lucerne, Switzerland.

Law, Social Movements and the Politics of the Commons

Cases from the Italian South

Veronica Pecile

Routledge
Taylor & Francis Group
LONDON AND NEW YORK

First published 2025
by Routledge
4 Park Square, Milton Park, Abingdon, Oxon OX14 4RN

and by Routledge
605 Third Avenue, New York, NY 10158

Routledge is an imprint of the Taylor & Francis Group, an informa business

A GlassHouse book

British Library Cataloguing-in-Publication Data
A catalogue record for this book is available from the British Library

Library of Congress Cataloging-in-Publication Data
Names: Pecile, Veronica, 1989- author.
Title: Law, social movements, and the politics of the commons : cases from the Italian South / Veronica Pecile.
Description: Abingdon, Oxon [UK] ; New York, NY : Routledge, 2025. | Includes bibliographical references and index.
Identifiers: LCCN 2024036706 (print) | LCCN 2024036707 (ebook) |
Subjects: LCSH: Commons--Political aspects--Italy, Southern. | Public domain--Italy, Southern. | Government property--Italy, Southern. | Right of property--Italy, Southern. | Social movements--Economic aspects--Italy, Southern.
Classification: LCC KKH3040 .P43 2025 (print) | LCC KKH3040 (ebook) | DDC 343.45/0209457--dc23/eng/20240813
LC record available at https://lccn.loc.gov/2024036706
LC ebook record available at https://lccn.loc.gov/2024036707

ISBN: 978-1-032-37102-3 (hbk)
ISBN: 978-1-032-37103-0 (pbk)
ISBN: 978-1-003-33532-0 (ebk)

DOI: 10.4324/9781003335320

Typeset in Sabon
by Taylor & Francis Books

Contents

Acknowledgements

This work began during my doctoral research at the École des Hautes Études en Sciences Sociales (EHESS) in Paris, which I conducted between 2015 and 2019. I am grateful to the Région Île-de-France for providing me with the funding for my doctoral contract and the research mobility grant to carry out the fieldwork. I also thank the EHESS for the scientific structure to which it gave me access during my doctoral studies, for the great range of courses it offered and for allowing me to spend a semester at the Center for the Study of Law and Society at the UC Berkeley School of Law. I wish to thank my two PhD supervisors, Paolo Napoli at the EHESS and Maria Rosaria Marella at the University of Perugia, for being such brilliant and patient mentors in all these years. Adalgiso Amendola and Mikhaïl Xifaras, as members of my PhD committee, gave me valuable suggestions to improve my dissertation and I am grateful to them. Michael Burawoy, Marianne Constable, Mia Fuller and Tony Platt were wonderful encounters during an unforgettable time in California that changed my life in all possible ways.

I am very grateful to David Kennedy and Arnulf Becker Lorca for their mentorship during my postdoctoral contract at the Institute for Global Law and Policy at Harvard Law School in 2021/22. I also thank Michele Tedeschini for his friendship and companionship during a strange year we spent together in Boston. As the pandemic raged and our lives became more and more isolated, discussing ideas at home, in seminar rooms and online gave me joy and hope.

During my postdoctoral fellowship at the Collegium Helveticum in Zurich in 2022/23, the book draft began to take shape. I am grateful to the Director, Sebastian Bonhoeffer, and the Head of the Academic Programs, Mario Wimmer, for leading the Collegium with care and respect for intellectual freedom. I am thankful to my research fellows in Zurich, Hannes Bajohr and Raffaela Kunz, for being great scholars and friends.

My thanks also go to Mariana Valverde for our inspiring encounter at the Law and Society Annual Conference in Lisbon in 2022 and to Vaios Karavas for supporting my research work at the Institute for Interdisciplinary Legal Studies at the Faculty of Law of the University of Lucerne since 2023.

I am very grateful for the support of the Swiss Institute in Rome in the academic year 2023/24. I would like to thank in particular the Director, Joëlle Comé, the Scientific Advisor, Maria Böhmer, the staff and my fellow residents, especially my friends Camilla Paolino and Léa Katharina Meier. Thank you for creating a place of friendship and love, a dream on earth, where life is sweet, and drafts get finished.

I had the opportunity to present on themes treated in this book on various occasions: at the "Legal Imaginations" Summer School of the University of Perugia in 2016; at the annual international workshop of the International Cultural Centre of Cerisy-la-Salle in 2017; at the Sciences Po Law School Doctoral Week in 2018; at the National Conference on Law and Society in Rome in 2020; at the International Conference on the Urban Commons at the University of Turin in 2021; at the research fellows' meetings of the Institute of Global Law and Policy at Harvard Law School in 2021/22; at the annual conference of the Law and Society Association in Lisbon in 2022; at the workshop on modern law and time I organised at the Collegium Helveticum in Zurich in 2022; at the workshop on law and climate change at the Istituto Svizzero in Rome in 2022. I am grateful to the organisers of these conferences and events and to the participants for their insightful comments and discussions.

Sections of the Introduction and of Chapters 1 and 2 were published in 2022 as 'Between urban commons and touristification: radical and conservative uses of the law in post-austerity Southern Italy' (*City – Analysis of Urban Change, Theory, Action* 6(26): 998–1011) and as 'Il sud, la pandemia e lo spirito del capitalismo italiano' on the *Lavoro Culturale* blog in 2020. An earlier version of Chapter 3 was published in 2021 as 'The Legal Field as a Battleground for Social Struggle: Reclaiming Law from the Margins' (*The Onati Socio-Legal Series* 11(6): 187–208). An alternative version of sections of Chapter 4 was published in 2023 in 'Belonging, Things and Time(s). Elements for a Spatio-Temporal Perspective on Law' (*The Italian Law Journal* 9(2): 681–695). Parts of the Conclusion were published in 'Between the "Southern Question" and the "Urban Question": the Struggle for Social Justice in Touristified Southern Italian Cities' (*Sens Public – Revue internationale et espace commun d'action et d'écriture*, 2024).

The ideas for this book would not exist without the great conversations I have had with my friends over the years. Serena Bassi, Federico Brandmayr, Giacomo Capuzzo, Sara Cavallo, Lorenzo Coccoli, Anna Montebugnoli, Lucia Rubinelli, Michele Spanò and Tara Zivkovic: thank you for being such great friends, generous human beings and luminous thinkers. I am grateful to all the people I met in Palermo – friends, activists, public servants – for the patience, time and trust they accorded me during my fieldwork. Their contributions, anonymised in the text, are the heart of this book, and I hope I made good use of them. Thanks to the series editor Colin Perrin for accepting my book proposal and for providing valuable insights throughout the writing process and to Naomi Round Cahalin for her support in the submission stage. Finally, thanks to my family – my parents, aunts, uncles and cousins – for being the most loud, quarrelsome, political, funny, loving crowd of my life.

Introduction

The commons under strain

The struggle for the commons in the 2010s

In the aftermath of the 2008 financial breakdown, mobilisations for the commons multiplied worldwide as a set of practices of resistance against the privatisation of resources and services carried out through austerity policies. In Western Europe, these measures greatly affected Southern countries and marked a renewal of the neoliberal economic and political project (Tulumello 2016). In opposition to austerity, groups of citizens and activists started claiming a right to occupy publicly and privately owned spaces and manage them as commons. Such a move was meant to promote the collective use and access of spaces and resources as well as to experiment with direct democracy and self-government. This political practice contributed to creating alternatives to the impasse of the classical forms of political mediation associated with the crisis of representative democracy (Dardot and Laval 2014; Sauvêtre 2016).

Alongside opposition to the neoliberal agenda, the movement for the commons involved ample legal experimentation. Activists participating in these mobilisations used the law counter-hegemonically, that is, to realise goals of socioeconomic justice and wealth redistribution in increasingly unequal societies. Experimentation with legal tools in the struggle for the commons in Europe included resorting to the courts to reclaim the collective access to spaces and resources, entering local governments to promote the self-government of urban areas, and adopting supranational legal instruments to foster public participation, such as the European Citizens' Initiative (Bailey and Mattei 2013).

The most radical instance of legal experimentation carried out by the movement for the commons consisted in rethinking the institution that in Western modern law regulates the relationship between individuals and things – property. Mobilisations for the commons succeeded in building a critique "in the field" of the conception of property that prevails in modern legal thought (Marella 2013a). However, it is important to stress that the commons did not emerge as a novel legal concept after the 2008 economic crisis. Instead, they have always been present in the modern legal repertoire as a marginal form of property, which frames the relations between individuals and things in a

DOI: 10.4324/9781003335320-1

radically different way than the predominant concept of private property – in which the owner's control over the thing is almost absolute, with few limits set by the law. The post-2008 crisis mobilisations have recovered and renewed these forms of ownership, which had been made almost unthinkable by the centuries-long alliance between modern law and capitalist exploitation. Against the absolute, individualistic and exclusive notion of property that is prevailing in modern capitalist societies, the movement for the commons practised an alternative vision of property, one in which the use of a space or thing is more important than the property title, the property interests of the non-owners and users gain relevance vis-à-vis those of the owners, and power is redistributed.

The Italian movement for *beni comuni* developed in a country in which different political forces had long been adopting policies to promote the privatisation of public companies and the sale of public assets on the market. These measures, promoted in the 1980s and 1990s, were strongly supported by legal experts who provided the theoretical justifications for such a reorganisation of property. The outcome of this operation, crucial to achieving market liberalisation, was a downsizing of the role of the state, which was no longer seen as the main deliverer of services but as a force behaving like any other market actor (Mattei and Quarta 2015).[1] The Italian movement for the commons emerging in the 2010s can be read as the culmination of an alliance of grassroots political subjects opposing this path of privatisation, which became even harsher with the government's adoption of austerity measures following the 2008 economic breakdown. A crucial episode that is often identified as marking the beginning of the movement was the "water referendum" of 2011, a public consultation in which citizens were asked whether they would approve the start of a process leading to the privatisation of water resources and services in the country. This event rapidly triggered a nationwide mobilisation against the privatisation targeting other resources, spaces and services. A movement emerged which saw diverse political realities and individuals gather around the idea that services and assets linked to the exercise of fundamental rights were *beni comuni* that should be collectively managed and enjoyed and removed from a public-private management that would submit them to the market logics.

An element that was crucial in determining the trajectory of the Italian movement for the commons was the synergy between activists and legal experts and practitioners who in those years were developing radical theoretical perspectives on property. The Rodotà Commission, a team of experts appointed by the Italian Ministry of Justice in 2007 to reform the articles of the national civil code regarding the regime of public goods, played a pivotal role in the reflections backing the activists' practice.

1 For a careful reconstruction of the Italian welfare transformation and downsizing over the past decades, see Giorgi (2022).

The Commission – named after its president, the prominent civil law scholar Stefano Rodotà – recognised that the existing legal regime posed no significant obstacle to the privatisation of public assets that had been unstoppable since the 1980s.[2] To reverse this trend, the group wrote a reform proposal based on the introduction of the commons as a legal concept into the civil code. In this draft, the commons (*beni comuni*) were defined as:

> things that express functional utilities for the exercise of fundamental rights and the free development of the person. The commons must be protected and safeguarded by the legal system, for the benefit of future generations as well. Owners of the commons may be public or private legal persons. In any case, their collective use must be guaranteed, within the limits and according to the modalities established by law. When the owners are public legal persons, the commons are managed by public entities and are placed out of commerce; their concession is permitted only in the cases provided for by law and for a limited duration, without the possibility of extension. The commons are, among others: rivers, streams and their sources; lakes and other waters; air; parks as defined by law, forests and wooded areas; high-altitude mountain areas, glaciers and perennial snows; lidos and

2 Stefano Rodotà had been focusing on the connections between property and the exercise of rights since the 1970s. Back then, at a time of thriving social democracy in the country, Rodotà focused on the issue of social control, namely, how the people could control the productive processes taking place in a given territory – for example, by deciding where to locate production hubs or how to develop urban planning. The proposed solution was to involve in decision-making all intermediate bodies, such as trade unions, workers' councils and neighbourhood associations. In the early twenty-first century, the Italian jurist will move on to suggest that given the weakening of these collective actors, it is the single citizen who should be in charge of opposing the exploitation of territories by reclaiming the individual exercise of fundamental rights (Rodotà 1974).

Rodotà had already addressed such issues in the 1960s, in an essay called *Note critiche in tema di proprietà* ("Critical notes on the theme of property"). Its focus was on the social function of property, a principle enshrined in Article 42 of the Italian Constitution ("Property is public or private. Economic assets may belong to the State, to public bodies or to private persons. Private property is recognised and guaranteed by the law, which prescribes the ways it is acquired, enjoyed and its limitations, in order to ensure its social function and make it accessible to all"). His argument was that the enshrinement of such a principle in the highest legal source marked the shift to a capitalist phase in which private property became the core of productive processes and had to be protected for this reason. The social function of property, in other words, was thought as a means to solve social conflict within the perimeter of property, and not outside of it (Rodotà 1960). In this reasoning, therefore, property is relativised and subordinated to the attainment of constitutional principles, which hold the person's full development and dignity as intrinsic values (Marella 2013b).

> stretches of coastline declared an environmental reserve; wildlife and protected flora; archaeological, cultural, environmental and other protected landscape areas.
>
> (Rodotà Commission Bill 2007)

This legal definition of the commons provided a powerful tool for social mobilisations for different reasons. First, it contains a distinction between the property title of a thing, which can be either public or private, and its function, which is tied to the way a community uses it. In other words, the property title ceases to be the most relevant aspect of ownership but is instead subordinated to the use (Spanò 2013). No matter who owns these resources, the law must guarantee their collective enjoyment within the limits established by law and also to the benefit of individuals who are not yet born and societies that do not yet exist – resumed in the reference to future generations. Second, this legal definition of the commons is helpful for activists because it allows them to reclaim the commons by linking them to the fulfilment of fundamental rights enshrined in national and supranational legal systems (Marella 2016). A system of diffused legal responsibility is thus established, one in which any individual who wants to reclaim a resource as a commons can act before a court to ensure its collective access, while it remains the state's responsibility to provide reparation for the harm that may be caused. A third important aspect of the legal definition of the commons introduced by the Rodotà Commission is that it includes no exhaustive list of what the commons are, although it is specified that natural resources and elements of the cultural and archaeological heritage can become commons. This means that things and resources are not commons per se, for some intrinsic qualities they bear, but they assume this status when a group activates their potential to become so by establishing a relationship of care and self-government with them. The emphasis is not on any alleged substance of the commons but rather on the relational dynamic from which they emerge. The commons do not preexist the groups taking care of them, but they emerge from a specific kind of praxis.

The Rodotà Commission's attempt to reform the civil code by introducing the commons as a legal concept did not go through, owing to the fall of the Prodi government in 2009, before the proposal could become law. This failure created an impasse in which a legal category was created without a surrounding legal regime supporting it (Grimonprez 2022). And yet, the Commission's legal definition of the commons had a massive impact not only on the doctrine but also on the jurisprudence in the following years. Some landmark judgments later recognised the neither public nor private character of certain things and resources, as a result of their use by communities. An example is the ruling in 2011 of the United Sections of the Italian Court of Cassation on the legal status of the fishing farms of the

Venetian lagoon. The judge acknowledged the existence of a right to a collective use of these resources:

> where property, regardless of the property title, is by its intrinsic connotations, in particular those of an environmental and landscape nature, intended for the realisation of welfare [...] it is to be considered [...] 'common', that is to say, regardless of the property title, instrumentally connected to the realisation of the interests of all citizens.
>
> (Italian Court of Cassation 2011)

Another example of how the legal definition of the commons proposed by the Rodotà Commission influenced case law is a ruling of the Civil Court of Rome, where the mobilisation of the commons developed in opposition to a widespread privatisation of cultural spaces that were being sold on the private market. In 2012 the Civil Court recognised the legitimacy of the occupation of the building of the former Cinema Palazzo by a group of art and cultural workers aimed at defending the space from private speculation that would have turned the space into a gambling hall:

> it must be noted that the interest underlying the demonstrative action consisting in the occupation of the building is political, not patrimonial or selfish: the demonstrators, who are still occupying the building today, oppose the destination that the applicant company would like to impose on it, claiming the preservation of the traditional 'cultural' vocation of the former Cinema Palazzo.
>
> (Tribunale di Roma 2012)

The definition of *beni comuni* and the interest of legal experts in theorising the commons also influenced the practice of social movements for several years to come. A case that epitomises the use of legal tactics by the Italian mobilisation for the commons was that of the Valle Theatre. This public building owned by the municipality of Rome was occupied in 2011 by a group of precarious art and cultural workers united to prevent its sale on the market. Throughout the occupation, the group acted with the support of a team of legal experts and scholars regularly part of the public assemblies through which the space was governed and gave advice on the legal "tricks" that could be used to continue governing the theatre as a commons – "neither public nor private" was the slogan adopted by the mobilisation. As the political and media discourse began to delegitimise the occupants, framing their practices as illegal, the activists decided to organise themselves as a legal subject and assumed the form of a private law foundation. Such a move provided them with the stability offered by the acquisition of a legal status, which would protect them from the shifting political orientations of the city administration in the future. While it is easy for a conservative municipality to get rid of an occupation, it is less so when occupants are a subject under private law. The Valle Theatre soon became the heart of a network of struggles for the commons multiplying all over the country, in which the self-government of spaces and practices of direct democracy were experimented, including the ex-Colorificio Toscano in Pisa, the ex-Asilo Filangieri in Naples and the Macao project in Milan (Mattei and Quarta 2015; Valli 2015; Varriale 2015).

The Italian movement for the commons developed mainly in urban contexts where the effects of the 2008 economic breakdown included a dramatic rise of poverty, unemployment and job insecurity, as well as a rapid decline in public welfare. Especially in crisis-ridden cities, *beni comuni* emerged as a set of diverse responses to the failures of traditional urban governance models founded on the alternative between private property and public intervention (Vercellone 2020). This model turned out to be incompatible with the residents' needs during economic recession and led to the pursuit of what can be considered as a contemporary understanding of the right to the city: the inhabitants' right not to be excluded from the city's social and economic structures and the urge to collectively manage spaces to realise emancipation and wealth redistribution (Lefebvre 1968; Harvey 2008; Foster 2019). Two elements made the movement innovative compared to previous urban experiences of occupation and squatting in the country. The first one was the political project at their core, namely the realisation of social and economic transformation through the self-government of spaces. The second one consisted in the uses of the law made by activists, making the movement different from previous mobilisations that were sceptical towards legal tools, seen as linked to the domination exerted by the ruling classes.

In Southern Italian cities, groups of citizens and activists reclaiming the commons acted within a network made up of other mobilisations which were simultaneously developing across the country, but also in response to context-specific conditions. The Italian South had been experiencing a long-standing state of social and economic crisis long before the 2008 breakdown, in terms of high rates of poverty and unemployment, absence of infrastructures and lack of public services (Di Feliciantonio and Aru 2018). As will emerge throughout the book, in these cities, the movement for the commons rose as a set of practices opposing the privatisation and neglect of public spaces in the post-2008 phase and then evolved into a struggle against processes undermining the right to use and access urban space, accelerated by the touristic turn of urban economies.

Outline of the argument

This book offers a novel perspective on the struggle for the commons that followed the 2008 financial breakdown from the angle of the Italian South. Its argument develops through two main points. First, it is argued that a governmental, top-down notion of the commons informed the discourses, norms and policies through which urban space was disciplined in the restructuring of societies and economies following the crisis. Second, the book explains that while the commons as a legal concept were deployed to regulate the urban space, grassroots practices were also being conducted in their name to achieve emancipation and wealth redistribution in increasingly unequal and touristified cities. To describe these two movements, I draw on the case of the Southern Italian mobilisations for *beni comuni* at a specific juncture, namely the shift that took place over the 2010s, and especially towards the end of the decade, to a tourism-based economic model adopted by the local elites as an antidote to the effects of the economic crisis, and the grassroots resistance that these transformations met.

The overall focus of the book is on the multiple dimensions of the commons as a political and legal concept and how they were developed by activists and local state actors alike in the Italian South after the 2008 crisis. Amidst the privatisation of resources, spaces and services and the intense activism opposing this process, theories and practices on the commons as a non-absolute and non-individualistic way of conceiving property have attracted a great deal of attention. This book starts out with a question: what did the commons look like in the cities of the Italian South, which differ in many respects from the urban ideal type of the global North? This means looking at how the commons as a concept and a practice have played out in the recent capitalist transformation of semi-peripheral contexts in Western Europe. It implies considering how the new processes of value extraction that have been reshaping cities of the Italian South have intertwined with ideas and experiences of the commons.

As I will explain throughout the book, along this trajectory of transformation the commons did not bear any emancipatory power per se – they were no magic wand capable of healing the staggering socio-economic inequalities of late capitalist cities – nor were they a tool solely in the hands of local elites to discipline societies and enable new modes of value extraction. Their role in the socio-economic metamorphosis of Southern Italian cities was instead an ambivalent one, and this ambiguity had much to do with how they were politically and legally imagined by a diverse array of subjects involved in the government of urban space. I will show how the commons can work both as capitalism's handmaiden – to use Nancy Fraser's expression – and as a repertoire of modes of resistance under the strain of neoliberal transformations.[3]

3 Fraser used the expression "capitalism's handmaiden" referring to white liberal feminism in an article appeared in *The Guardian* in 2013 which summarised the main points of her book *Fortunes of Feminism: From State-Management Capitalism to Neoliberal Crisis* (Fraser 2013a; 2013b).

On the one hand, in post-crisis Italian cities, many of the political projects pursued by the local elites converged around an idea, that of disciplining and regulating urban space to make it more suitable for tourism. At the core of this vision was a governmental, top-down idea of the commons, used to discipline both urban space and the citizens who are supposed to take care of it. The active citizen thus emerged as a new subjectivity bearing the moral duty of looking after the city following values of legality and participation and replacing an increasingly absent welfare state. While the emergence of this new citizen has been reconstructed by studies focusing on Northern Italy, no such analysis has been conducted to explore how this transformation took place in Southern Italian societies.[4]

This mutation of spaces and subjectivities in the cities of the Italian South has not been linear and has been met by resistance. During the 2010s, grassroots practices of self-government in the Italian *Mezzogiorno* emerged which did not draw on a governmental idea of the commons, but on a transformative one based on a radical critique of property. The movement for the commons in Italy was capable of contesting the predominant form of private property in which the owner's interests prevail on those of non-owners, users and passers-by. The practice of activists in cities like Palermo and Naples allowed for the reemergence of a marginalised conceptualisation of ownership from the layers of Western legal thought. Property is no longer the name of an individualistic, exclusive and almost absolute bond between the owner and the thing, but a tie connecting owners, non-owners and things – a bond that allows for the redistribution of access to spaces as well as of the wealth created by their use.

The case of commons in the Italian South reveals the co-existence of two movements based on radically different ideas of what *beni comuni* are – tools for enclosing or socialising urban space, restraining or expanding its use. This book thus provides a novel framework to examine how diverse and conflicting ideas of the commons – a concept that has been at the forefront of socio-legal studies for a couple of decades now – are at play in late capitalist scenarios, expressing different and, at times, even clashing political projects concerning cities and society at large. It explores how the neoliberalisation of economies and societies can take place not just in spite, but also in the name of the commons, and how uses of law – made by citizens, activists, state actors, private subjects – are of crucial importance in this process. It also highlights how despite attempts of co-optation, the political and legal imagination of the mobilisations reclaiming the commons is far from being tamed and is paving the way for legal regimes in which alternative forms of property can be envisaged, especially as tourism disrupts cities in the Italian South and elsewhere.

4 I am referring to the anthropological inquiry carried out by Andrea Muehlebach in neoliberal Lombardy which will be mentioned throughout the book.

Concepts

Legal technique

The first area of studies to which this book aims to contribute is the field of socio-legal studies, and in particular a broad strain of literature that adopts a critical and ethnographic perspective on legal phenomena. In order to develop an analysis of the commons in the Italian South, this book focuses on concrete practices carried out under the label of *beni comuni* in this region and revises existing theories in the light of these experiences. Scholars have long been stressing how the observation of "actually existing commons" can enrich the vast literature on the subject in fields such as legal theory, sociology and urban geography (Eizenberg 2012). This analysis can illuminate how neoliberal rationality – the mode of structuring and organising conducts in contemporary capitalist systems – varies according to the different economic, social and cultural scenarios in which it develops (Dardot and Laval 2014). In accordance with Wendy Brown, I consider neoliberalism as a peculiar, yet "inconsistent and differentiated" reason that reshapes every aspect of life, whose elements concur to transform the political character of democracy's founding elements into economic ones, thereby hampering the foundations of democracy (Brown 2015: 17–20). Focusing on actually existing commons also means putting into practice Aihwa Ong's intuition about the need to adopt an ethnographic perspective to grasp how market, sovereignty and citizenship are articulated in different scenarios affected by neoliberal transformations (Ong 2006).

This book is a contribution to this theoretical perspective, which explores contemporary legal phenomena without looking for all-encompassing theories and integrates it with an approach to law studied as a technique. In the formulation by French legal historian Yan Thomas in his genealogical work on Roman law, the idea of legal technique refers to law's capacity to function as a "machine of abstraction of social reality" (Spanò 2015: 89) – as a set of tools that are constructed through procedure and result from the concrete acts of institutions. The peculiar power of law is precisely that of instituting – of simultaneously naming and disciplining relations among individuals as well as between individuals and things – in one single gesture (Thomas 1978). The act of instituting is not speculation but a concrete process after which reality is no longer the same. In it, the jurist manages to

> isolate the sequence of frames that make up the shape of reality in such a way that, once the process is complete, it is no longer possible to go back because, in the eyes of the jurist, the recodification of people, things, actions and functions that follows that shaping has produced a concrete abstraction that instantly supplants the empirical datum.
>
> (Napoli 2023: 450)

Embracing this idea of legal technique means adopting an approach to law that is materialist and structuralist. First, it is materialist in the sense that the analysis does not start from a pre-given set of concepts but develops by drawing on concrete practices that have a significant legal dimension, and from such practices tries to extrapolate the concepts – for instance, property or the commons. Observing grassroots practices of reclaiming the commons can thus be an exploration into the transformation of legal forms in contemporary societies. Second, the adopted approach is structuralist in that all relations – between individuals, but also between individuals and things – are conceived as caught up in law, i.e., entangled in a web of institutional relations. This is different from thinking of norms as emerging spontaneously from the level of actors, as posited by some sociological and anthropological approaches to law. Instead, it means considering all things and subjects as produced through the acts of institutions – as normatively built. The story of the Southern Italian commons can thus be a touchstone for examining how distinct conceptions of the commons correspond to differing uses of legal forms deployed to realise diverse political projects.

Considering law as a technique has another important implication, namely, that of mitigating the widespread hostility that persists among social scientists towards the law. As Thomas pointed out, it enables to understand the history of law and its forms as part of a broader history, the one of the techniques through which modern societies have been shaped (Thomas 2002). It allows one to abandon the emphasis on the repressive side of law and to focus on its descriptive side, the one in which definitions for the forms of social life are offered – in other words, private law. It means to acknowledge that each relationship passes through private legal forms – contracts, property, torts – which mediate everything we do and function as the infrastructure of social life (Spanò 2022). As I will explain throughout the book, different configurations of such forms imply different redistributive effects concerning the resources and power at stake. The commons as a peculiar form of ownership can end up reproducing an absolute and individualistic concept of property; but they can also envisage a non-proprietary ownership, a way to institute relations through which the property interests of non-owners prevail and use emerges as a new paradigm for governing things, spaces and territories.

Legal discourse

In the book, law will be explored not only as a technique but also as a discourse. Following Foucault, I refer to the latter as a historically contingent social system capable of producing knowledge and meaning and "practices that systematically form the object of which they speak" (Foucault

1969: 49). As I will explain, the story of the Southern Italian commons is useful for understanding how in the post-2008 crisis phase, discourses circulating in the public sphere and establishing the criteria for acting legitimately within it played an important role in taming the emancipatory potential of the commons and partly neutralising it into a governmental device. If the commons could become a tool contributing to capitalist reorganisation, that happened through norms, policies and cultural representations informed by a specific discursive order made up of two main elements: legality as equated to the respect of existing legal rules and participation reduced to the top-down involvement of some groups of worthy citizens into government.

The discursive order of legality and participation that informed public life in Italian cities and influenced the trajectory of the commons in the 2010s is the result of specific social and political elements steadily rooted in Italy's and global recent history. As will be discussed in this book, a discourse reducing legality to the respect of formal legality emerged as one of the outcomes of the state reaction against political violence conducted in the country since the late 1970s. Whether fully embraced or critically reinterpreted, legality delimited what could be said and done in the realm of public action and therefore had a major impact on the mobilisations for the commons. As for participation, I will explore how discourses promoting participatory processes – based on the formal involvement of some groups of citizens in the government of cities and territories – were adopted at the EU level as a panacea for the crisis of democratic mechanisms in the post-2008 phase and had a great influence on policies and legislations adopted at supranational and national levels.

The translation of such discourses into policy and legal tools implied not only a restructuring of how urban space is governed but also the rise of a new subjectivity. In her ethnography of the restructuring of Lombardy's economy in the early 2000s, Andrea Muehlebach highlights how an "ethical citizen" emerges as an individual with a strong moral posture in charge of providing welfare through volunteer work (Muehlebach 2012). In this book, I argue that the local version of this subjectivity in the Italian South is the active citizen, as it is legally defined in hundreds of municipal regulations on the government of the urban commons adopted since the mid-2010s. This individual is deemed to realise legality and participation through an efficient self-management of public spaces conducted in the name of a civic notion of the commons. The active citizen is the bulwark of a modern civil society defined along parameters of legality and participation, which is constructed as the main state's ally in disciplining urban space.

What lies outside of this realm in Southern Italian cities are individuals that can be described through the concept of political society as it was developed in postcolonial studies, which in turn continued a reflection started by Antonio Gramsci (Chatterjee 2004). A consistent urban population accessing the economy outside of formal state/market channels, which reclaims rights and citizenship without resorting to the discourses of legality and participation – this is what the political society looks like in contemporary cities of the Italian South. Left out of the official socio-economic structures, this population provides the symbolic core of the new urban economies based on a tourism of folklore, authenticity and everyday life, exotic and palatable for tourists and investors alike. Its members – their livelihood, imaginary and bodies in the urban space – are the source of these cities' attractiveness and the object of an ever-renewed process of reinvention of tradition (Hobsbawm and Ranger 1992). At the same time, the political society of the Italian South is also the one whose very survival is threatened in increasingly unequal cities. As we will see, legal instruments can be adopted at the city level to provide them with social and economic protection and to recognise a subjectivity that has different characteristics than those of the moral citizen who diligently looks after a disciplined urban space. These tools succeed in reframing legality and participation in a counter-hegemonic way: the former as a class-conscious political project of wealth redistribution and the latter as the involvement of the most marginalised in a radical urban politics committed to direct democracy and socioeconomic justice. Studying the trajectory of the commons in the Italian South thus allows one to explore how different discourses of legality and participation preside over the creation of new subjectivities that are made and negotiated through legal means.

Italy's "Southern Question", or the spirit of Italian capitalism

This book aims at bridging insights from socio-legal studies with those of an expanding interdisciplinary field that has explored how the Italian South is made and remade – from a discursive, cultural, political, legal point of view. This has been the scope of scholars in Italian studies, who have increasingly used the tools of historical research, postcolonial studies critical theory and cultural studies to provide a critical analysis of Italy as a transnational object, namely, as the result of an interaction of cultural practices and histories taking place globally (Burdett et al. 2020; Bassi et al. 2023; Lombardi-Diop 2023). By providing an in-depth exploration of the mobilisations for the commons in the Italian South, this book offers a reading of the commons through the conceptual lens provided by the so-called "Southern Question". The "Southern Question" is not just the structural imbalance in socio-economic terms between the North and the South of the country, which has been reproduced through laws, policies and discourses since national unification in 1861 and has been radically interpreted first by Gramsci. Certainly, it is the framing of the Italian South by members of the political and intellectual elite as "under-developed, backward and ultimately different from Northern and Central

Italy" (Giglioli 2017: 411). However, as Goffredo Polizzi has highlighted, the Southern Question is also a "site of interrogation", a crucial debate that, ever since its appearance in the eighteenth and nineteenth centuries, has provided a vantage point to investigate the making of the Italian national project and its intertwinement with global trajectories of capitalist modernisation (Polizzi 2022: 1). In this work, I look at the Southern Italian commons as a prism through which to critically conduct such an interrogation in the late capitalist phase following the 2008 economic crisis with its profound restructuring of societies and economies. As I will explain, the renovation of Southern Italian urban economies in a touristic sense is deeply entangled with the Southern Question and the commons of the Italian South provide a litmus test for understanding the rhythm, the features and even the inconsistencies of the neoliberal transformation occurring in this region.

A thesis of this book is then that the Southern otherness, embodied by its political society, is the authentic spirit of Italian capitalism. The alterity of the Italian *Mezzogiorno* – constructed as backward and underdeveloped vis-à-vis the allegedly modern and progressed North – is not simply a discourse that has been adopted by national elites ever since Italian unification. It is also a material arrangement of socioeconomic disparities that has been produced and reproduced at different stages of Italian history. "Orientalism in one country" is the formula introduced by Jane Schneider to describe this trajectory of Italian racialisation and the asymmetry of power relations it has fostered (Gibson 1998). In the Italian national project, the South as a margin of modernity has been formed and reformed at each historical juncture of crisis – at every stage of capitalist restructuring – by an ever-renewing interweaving of discourses, policies, cultural representations created by intellectuals, statesmen, institutions and all the subjects that produce hegemony in Gramscian terms – an organisation of consensus percolating from the dominant social classes to other social groups (Gramsci 1977).

There are three main moments in which the otherness of the Italian South has been renewed. The first one is the period following national unification in 1861, a time in which the anthropologist Alfredo Niceforo wrote in an essay on the *Mezzogiorno* titled "Barbarian contemporary Italy" (*L'Italia barbara contemporanea*) that "here Italy has a high mission to accomplish and a colony to civilise" (Niceforo 2012). At that historical moment, the national elites' intent was to connect the newly unified peninsula, which included vast areas of latifundia in the Southern region, to the continental capitalist system. Intellectuals and statesmen were playing their part in constructing the ideological climate for this change, insisting that the state should adopt the most modern practices of government to manage peoples who recalled "the savages of Americas", as Leopoldo Franchetti wrote in a 1876 report on the political and administrative conditions of Sicily (Franchetti 1985). This first construction of Southerners as the main "internal other" of the Italian nation was ratified by the introduction of national statistics and by infamous theories inspired by scientific positivism concerning their supposed biological inferiority, such as the ones of Cesare Lombroso (Gibson 1998; Patriarca 1998).[5] Important voices rose against this essentialist and racist construction of the South. For instance, Filippo Turati and Napoleone Colajanni, both socialists, stressed how the high crime rates in the South that were reported as reasons to impose order were due not to biological and racial causes but to historical and social factors, such as structural poverty and lack of access to education and work. These were the theoretical and political foundations of *meridionalismo*, a thinking critically reinterpreting the specificity of the Italian South vis-à-vis the rest of the country that would exert a major influence on Gramsci (Minichiello 1997).

A second crucial moment of reinvention of the Southern alterity in opposition to the modern and capitalist North was the post-war period. The fuel of the *miracolo italiano* – the national economic boom of the 1950s and 1960s – was the low-cost labour provided by the Southern migrants working in northern factories. As Paul Ginsborg writes, high levels of unemployment in the South combined with a large need of workers in the Northern factories resulted in very low wages and created a scenario in which the increase in productivity was accompanied by a disproportionate rise in the exploitation of workers (Ginsborg 1990). The Cassa del Mezzogiorno, a public institution created in 1950 to foster the economic development of the South, did not succeed in solving systemic problems such as the lack of infrastructure, poverty and unemployment. Not even the land reform, which in the post-war period was supposed to calm tensions in the rural areas and revitalise the social fabric, was able to redress the socio-economic imbalances in the South and slow down emigration to the North. Against ideals of progress as linear economic development everywhere, the Italian case shows how imbalance is consubstantial to the advance of capitalism and is just one among many patterns of accumulation.

The marginalisation of the South within the national project was justified by moral evaluations and intellectual reconstructions produced not only inside but also outside the country. Works such as Edward Banfield's *The Moral Basis of a Backward Society* became a theoretical reference for

5 This process of internal racialisation precedes and accompanies the Italian colonial project, in which the dynamics of othering is projected outside of the nation state onto the colonised people. Critical studies on Italian colonialism have been multiplying over the past decades and entered a public debate that has traditionally been oblivious to the history of the Italian empire. See at least Ben-Ghiat and Fuller (2008), Del Boca (1992), Mazzacane (2006) and Srivastava (2016).

anyone who believed in the inconsolable backwardness of the Italian South (Banfield 1958). Still in the 1990s, political scientist Robert Putnam could write that while in Northern Italy people acted like citizens belonging to a modern civil society, in the South they reasoned like the subjects of a decrepit feudal system (Putnam 1994). In the post-war period, the imperative of Southern modernisation was realised in spectacular fashion under the watchful eyes of international observers. One example was the special law imposing the evacuation of Matera in 1952, which forced the city's inhabitants to leave the Sassi – the infernal crater, as Carlo Levi called them in his novel *Christ Stopped at Eboli* – that had been declared unhealthy and uninhabitable by the public authorities. Ernesto de Martino denounced the culturalist approach of the project carried out by the Christian Democratic government with the support of US consultants. Against this blatant orientalism, his research revealed how the transformations of Southern societies in those years were tightly linked to the economic development occurring in the rest of the country and shaped by a constant comparison with normative models of progress (Forgacs 2014).

The otherness of the Italian South was reconstituted for a third time in the neoliberal phase beginning in the late 1980s and continuing today. This was a stage of decreasing public investment and deregulation of entire economic sectors, responding to the imperative of joining the European Monetary Union and being part of a global order in which liberalisation was key to achieve economic integration. The Cassa del Mezzogiorno was abolished without ever having succeeded in ensuring an effective redistribution of resources and a time of slow and inexorable disinvestment in the Southern regions began (Rossi 2019). In this book, I argue that an important aspect of the still ongoing neoliberal phase that the trajectory of the Southern Italian commons shows is how the marginality of the South is no longer framed as an obstacle to modernisation but has become the engine of capitalist transformation. The construction of the Italian South as a touristic destination – in some cases a reconstruction, such as in the case of Naples, which has been for a long time a Grand Tour attraction made as a cultural object by an external and orientalist gaze – draws on a precise dynamic of accumulation, in which value is extracted from the authentic and folkloric character of the inhabitants' livelihood. This touristic monoculture is detrimental and even disastrous for society in the medium and long term, as it encourages real estate speculation, exploits those who are already marginalised and does not create permanent mechanisms for wealth redistribution. This is the great transformation that the movement for the commons in the Italian South found itself confronted with and to which, as I will explain, it has responded by adopting different discursive, political and legal tactics.

Methodology

A critical and materialist approach to modern legal forms

Methodologically, the book develops as a reflection on the commons from multiple disciplinary perspectives, while relying upon material emerging from fieldwork that is used to challenge and deepen existing theories on the topic. As for the theoretical component, I draw on insights from private legal theory which in recent years have consolidated a critical and genealogical approach to modern legal forms. In this field, there has been growing attention to the study of alternative forms of ownership existing within and outside the modern legal tradition as well as an increasing focus on the commons as a legal concept expressing a non-absolute and non-exclusive idea of ownership in which the use is more relevant than the property title. This attention towards the commons has developed through an eclectic methodological posture, i.e., in dialogue with diverse strands of literature exploring the connections between alternative forms of property and the social and economic contexts in which they have been imagined and practised (Davies 2012; Cooper 2014; Marella 2017). In this book, I adopt this eclecticism while embracing three main commitments emerging from recent strands of critical legal studies. The first is to undertake an ethnographic approach to law, namely, one that concentrates on how normativities are produced at a grassroots level. This is particularly important in a phase like the one following the 2008 economic breakdown, in which social movements and civil society widely resorted to legal tactics to advance claims for social justice and wealth redistribution (Bailey and Mattei 2013; Rizzini Ansari and Amadeo 2022). The second is the critique of the subject-owner as it is conventionally framed in modern legal thought to find legal ways for recognising a collective, assembled, "not-one" subject, which relates to things in a non-proprietary way (Spanò 2022). This kind of subject is emerging in recent scholarly discussions and case law introducing the rights of nature and other tools that provide the natural world with personhood and contest the anthropocentrism of Western law (Grear 2015; RiverOfLife et al. 2021; Petersmann 2023). The third commitment I draw on is the critical scholarship focusing on law's materiality, specifically on how norms are produced not only in the realm of human and social activities but of nonhumans and objects as well (Vismann 2008; Grabham 2016; Davies 2022).

These three perspectives provide the foundations for the critical socio-legal methodology adopted in this book. I do not intend critique merely as a set of theoretical efforts aimed at understanding the single elements that make up a singular social dynamic, such as the one of the Southern Italian commons. With Judith Butler, I contend that critique has a positive dimension at its heart, which is often overlooked by those who deem it as a purely negative posture and consists of the interrogation of taken-for-granted presumptions in order to imagine a different world (Butler 2009; 2024). I understand critique thus conceived as a specific way of conducting a materialist history of legal concepts. This means two essential things. First, it implies to embrace a materialist idea of praxis, namely, to see political practice as capable of producing thought and not as a set of deeds translating pre-existing ideas into action (Napoli 2023). Second, it means recognising "the abstract and formal character of legal concepts, their instituting performance and their virtual antagonism" (Spanò 2022: 22). The main focus is, then, on the products of law's quintessential activity, i.e., instituting. These are a set of forms and abstractions that are superposed to social reality in an imperfect way and while not exhausting the infinite possibilities of the real, have the power of shaping and generating it. The focus of this book is on property as one of the main private legal forms and on the manifold shapes it can assume despite the hegemony, in Western modern thought, of its absolute, individualistic and exclusive conception.

Thinking through the case, or, beyond the case study

Adopting a critical and materialist approach to legal forms as the one just described has a further methodological implication that has to do with the object of the inquiry. Such a perspective enables one to escape a common paradigm in social sciences, that of the case study. It allows to challenge the idea, implicit in it, that a truth can be summarised in a theoretical concept derived from social facts of an emblematic force. I instead believe, with Mariana Valverde, that socio-legal scholars should escape the "case study" language and its universalist pretensions and abandon the quest for greater truths, as "ideas are means to the end of understanding our world as concretely as is possible" (Valverde 2015: 2).

Getting rid of the case study poses a problem: which should be the object of any socio-legal inquiry, such as this one? My guess is that the case, as conceived in the *casuistique* developed in legal history by Yan Thomas and Paolo Napoli, provides a valuable alternative. The case is to law what the field, the *terrain*, is to social sciences, with one important difference: while the field is a part of external reality that is subject to human inquiry, the case is not external to the legal procedure but is created by it, through the ways in which the jurists qualify social reality. While for the social sciences the field – and the case study constructed by extracting elements from it – has the function of producing a truth that validates or rejects the theoretical hypothesis, the case reflects how legal forms act upon and shape reality, but this is only one among the many ways in which they could be used: in different circumstances, the same forms could be activated in entirely different ways, or they could be reinvented altogether. This element of latency of the legal forms will emerge clearly in the experience of the Southern Italian commons. In this story, we will see not only how different conceptions of the property form can be used to pursue manifold visions of society, but also how diverse mobilisations taking place across different cities and contexts are held together by what appears as a horizontal fabric, a sort of cloth made of different, interwoven uses of law which, if regarded from outside, shows how it is property itself that is being remade through praxis. This approach is at odds not only with the case study paradigm of the social sciences, with its implicit claim to generalisation, but also to the conventional case method pursued in legal studies and theorised by Langdell, in which the rule is elaborated starting from the precedent in a vertical and hierarchical way. What unites the cases examined in this book is a fundamental question to which they try to respond: how to find shared rules for the collective use and access to things and spaces in a situation of social and economic crisis? This book is also an account of a gap, of a hiatus between the social reality of mobilisations, municipalities and private actors on the one hand and the domain of normativities on the other, of this intermediate region made up of unstable and ephemeral bonds between individuals, things and actions, which is the ultimate realm of law (Napoli 2024).

Ethnographic research

I spent a total of eight months in Palermo between Spring 2016 and Winter 2019 conducting field research during my PhD. In this part of the work, I borrowed and adapted methods belonging to sociology and anthropology for my research, although this book does not have the ambition of being either a sociological or an anthropological inquiry. It remains an exploration of the commons as a politico-legal concept which draws on a concrete analysis aimed at complicating and challenging several theoretical aspects of this notion.

In the course of fieldwork, I deployed qualitative research methods: participant observation to public assemblies and other activities organised by the mobilisations reclaiming *beni comuni*, a collection of written and digital materials produced by activists and 15 semi-structured interviews conducted with different subjects involved in the trajectory of the mobilisation in many ways – as militants, association members, components of Catholic organisations, social workers, public servants, users of regenerated spaces, researchers. My first stay in Palermo took place one year after the start of the research, a time in which I examined the vast scholarship on the commons in legal philosophy, private law and socio-legal studies as well as the viewpoint provided by anthropological and sociological literature on neoliberalism and austerity. During all my stays in Palermo, I lived in the historic centre, at first for logistic reasons, and observed the practices conducted under the label of commons in that area. I later understood that limiting my observation to the central part of the city was a methodologically appropriate choice, as it allowed me to closely observe the rampant urban and social transformation affecting the *centro storico* and turning it into an increasingly monotonous touristic economy.

The core of the ethnographic research are the observations and interviews providing the backbone of Chapter 1. These interlocutions, although varying in duration and formality, were conducted in an open and conversational style, without setting any pre-constituted direction for the exchange that followed and are all completely anonymised in the text (Rositi 1993). The act of interviewing reminded me of how building human relationships and the art of listening, which are key to oral history, are crucial for building solid and critical socio-legal studies (Portelli 2009). In the course of these conversations, I never aspired to be impartial and distant from the interviewees; on the contrary, I benefited from the advantages of conducting ethnography from a politically engaged position, with people whose efforts to confront the crisis from below, through practices of solidarity-building and resistance to the extraction of value from people's everyday practices, I fully shared (Chatterton et al. 2008; Arampatzi 2017).

Outline of chapters

This book is made of an introduction, four chapters and a conclusion. **Chapter 1** explores some of the mobilisations for the commons that took place in Southern Italian cities, drawing on fieldwork I conducted in Palermo. I look at three groups of grassroots practices: the reclaiming of culture as a commons realised through the occupation and self-government of cultural spaces by precarious art workers and other activists; the urban renewal of public spaces conducted by citizen groups in areas abandoned to neglect; and a process of urban regeneration initiated by activists in an open-air market area of a popular neighbourhood affected by a fast touristic transformation. What these diverse groups of activists and citizens reclaiming urban space share is a resort to a vocabulary of the commons to legitimise their practices. In some cases, groups pursuing the commons sought and found a terrain of negotiation with the local public actor and succeeded in changing the norms establishing how the concerned spaces should be used and accessed. The rules resulting from this interaction enshrined different ideas of the commons as a legal concept, some of them transformative – connected to self-government, direct democracy and wealth redistribution – and others conservative – to order and govern urban space in a disciplinary way.

Even when no negotiation took place about the rules establishing the allowed uses of spaces, law was omnipresent at the discursive and symbolic level. I focus on legality and participation as two discursive orders establishing the criteria for public action in Italian cities in the post-2008 crisis phase. I also concentrate on the collective subject embodying such ideals into one consistent identity, namely a civil society that collaborates with the state to manage urban space and enact a civic, governmental and moral idea of the commons. These discourses not only had the power to influence public debate and action but also had an impact on the making of rules on how urban space should be used. A public law regulation for the shared management of the commons has been adopted in hundreds of Italian cities since 2014 and provides today an important legal framework for city administrations in the whole country. At the core of this instrument is a subject, the active citizen, deemed to act as the responsible individual in charge for the care of the commons. The chapter then moves on to analysing what remains beyond a civil society defined according to such traits. The postcolonial notion of political society is introduced as useful to describe the population that does not fit in the discourses of legality and participation and nevertheless reclaims a right to use and access public space, also by mobilising the commons as a political and legal concept.

Chapters 2, 3 and 4 draw on the story of the Palermo's commons outlined in Chapter 1 to explore a set of political and legal philosophical issues emerging from it. **Chapter 2** departs from the observed practices of grassroots reclaiming of urban space to sketch the features of a politics of the commons that remains largely unpredicted by the existing literature. The main argument is that the commons act as an empty signifier in Laclau's terms, namely as an umbrella claim able to encompass diverse social demands in late capitalist contexts undergoing profound urban and socioeconomic transformations. In the Italian South, such a malleability of the commons made them available to work both for and against the nonlinear, contradictory and yet seemingly unstoppable neoliberal restructuring of societies and economies. This dynamic, in which different actors compete over the uses of urban space by resorting to diverse, at times clashing visions of the commons, makes the construction of a consistent legal regime of *beni comuni* a problematic goal. The chapter also focuses on the traits of the groups reclaiming spaces and resources as commons, arguing that they differ in significant ways from the romantic ideal type of community posited by several strains in critical scholarship. Redefining the commons, and the communities taking care of them, means also to reconceive the very meaning of their autonomy. Rather than acting along the "neither-public-nor-private" mantra that accompanied the first phase of the movement for *beni comuni*, groups reclaiming the commons are deeply entangled with both state and market spheres and conduct their practices not outside, but within and among these structures. I then contextualise the politics of the Southern Italian commons in the 2010s within the reconfiguration of urban space brought about by the adoption of a touristic economic model by local elites. An important means to carry out this transformation consisted of public policies on realms such as urban renovation and markets' regulation that had at their core a governmental notion of the commons. Finally, I contextualise the trajectory of the observed mobilisations for the commons within the late capitalist transformations of the Italian South, focusing on how the political society's everyday life is the main target of contemporary processes of value extraction. The alleged backwardness and otherness of the Southern Italian popular classes vis-à-vis the North – a trait which has been produced and reproduced through discursive, policy and legal means throughout the history of modern Italy – is no longer an obstacle to accumulation: on the contrary, it is made visible and commodified in ad hoc spaces and provides the core logic for the touristic reorganisation of cities. In this metamorphosis, the commons and the groups reclaiming them played a complex role, being at the same time a frequent object of co-optation from the side of the state and an engine of new practices of urban resistance opposing the detrimental effects of tourism. The trajectory of the Southern Italian commons thus provides a litmus test to understand how the neoliberalisation of the Italian South proceeded in the post-crisis decade of the 2010s and offers hints to reflect on similar transformations occurring in other semi-peripheral and peripheral contexts at the same stage.

In **Chapter 3** I reconsider the story of the Southern Italian commons outlined in the first chapter from another theoretical perspective, namely, that of socio-legal studies and legal sociology. The starting point is an exploration of the mistrust towards the uses of law that has been widespread among critical theorists and activists alike, although tactical uses of legal tools by social movements have been observable for decades, with the movement for the commons providing an important example. I attempt to trace an intellectual genealogy of this scepticism in some situated readings of Marx and Foucault's work, which tend to provide a partial interpretation of their thinking, by artificially separating the realms of law and politics and conflating law with the repressive end of power. I then turn to critical legal studies and in particular to the idea of law as inherently indeterminate and open to different political projects – the thesis advanced by the "crits" of law as politics all the way down. Adopting this perspective, it emerges how legal forms that have conventionally been used to ensure subordination and exclusion can be used counter-hegemonically to realise emancipatory visions of society. Among such forms, property stands out for its potential to be used for redistributing access to spaces and wealth in increasingly unequal cities. Upon this premise, I move on to outline a non-exhaustive array of legal "tricks" – of uses of the law that can be made to protect the property interests of the marginalised and advance non-proprietary claims over the urban space and that are available both in the private and the public law realms, focusing on community land trusts and civic uses. I conclude the chapter by focusing on a growing trend in legal theory and practice, namely the attribution of legal personhood to non-human entities such as parts of the natural world. I highlight the potential of this approach in decentring the modern legal subject as well as its limits, namely the possible reaffirming of the extractivist vocation that has been accompanying the use of modern legal forms throughout capitalist modernity. In order to institute the commons, it is not enough to turn things, spaces and natural resources into legal subjects: rather, I suggest to focus on those legal instruments that enable the recognition of a subject that is not-one, collective, assembled – that allow, in one formula, to institute the collective.

Chapter 4 returns to the mobilisations for the commons outlined in Chapter 1 to conduct a final exercise in legal abstraction. It looks at the Southern Italian commons from the vantage point of legal theory, and in particular property theory, to delineate the features of a legal regime of the commons. Drawing on the mobilisations outlined in Chapter 1, it sketches a model of abstraction built on a critical reinterpretation of two forms that are central to modern legal thought. These are belonging, which will here be conceived as broader than property, and things, considered not as pre-given to but built through legal technique. It identifies them by adopting an approach to modern law that is at once critical and historical: critical because it departs from a set of questions concerning the impact of the Southern Italian commons on property as a legal form; and historical in the sense of based on a genealogical approach to property, aimed at retrieving marginal ways in which it has been conceived away from its predominant form. This final chapter thus complements the previous analyses of the philosophical and sociological implications of the Southern Italian commons focusing on the theoretical legal implications of their reappearance. The aim is to trace in them the foundations of an alternative property regime through which the collective is instituted.

References

Arampatzi, Athina. 2017. The Spatiality of Counter-Austerity Politics in Athens, Greece: Emergent "Urban Solidarity Spaces". *Urban Studies* 54(9): 2155–2171.

Bailey, Saki and Ugo Mattei. 2013. Social Movements As Constituent Power: The Italian Struggle for The Common. *Indiana Journal of Global Legal Studies* 20(2): 965–1013.

Banfield, Edward C. 1958. *The Moral Basis of a Backward Society*. Glencoe, IL: Free Press.

Bassi, Serena, Loredana Polezzi, and Giulia Riccò. 2023. Introduction: Critical Issues in Transnational Italian Studies. *Forum Italicum* 57 (2): 273–288.

Ben-Ghiat, Ruth and Mia Fuller. 2008. *Italian Colonialism*. Basingstoke: Palgrave Macmillan.

Brown, Wendy. 2015. *Undoing the Demos: Neoliberalism's Stealth Revolution*. New York: Zone Books.

Burdett, Charles, Loredana Polezzi and Marco Santello. 2020. *Transnational Italian Studies*. Liverpool: Liverpool University Press.

Butler, Judith. 2009. Critique, Dissent, Disciplinarity. *Critical Inquiry* 35(4): 773–795.

Butler, Judith. 2024. Fascist Passions (lecture held at the University of Bologna on 7 May 2024).

Chatterjee, Partha. 2004. *The Politics of the Governed: Popular Politics in Most of the World*. New York: Columbia University Press.

Chatterton, Paul, Duncan Fuller and Paul Routledge. 2008. Relating Action to Activism: Theoretical and Methodological Reflections. In *Participatory Action Research Approaches and Methods: Connecting People, Participation and Place*, edited by Sara Louise Kindon, Mike Kesby and Rachel Pain, pp. 216–222. London: Routledge.

Cooper, Davina. 2014. *Everyday Utopias: The Conceptual Life of Promising Spaces*. Durham, NC: Duke University Press.

Dardot, Pierre and Christian Laval. 2014. *The New Way of the World: On Neoliberal Society*. London: Verso Books.

Davies, Margaret. 2012. Persons, Property, and Community. *Feminists@law* 2(2).

Davies, Margaret. 2022. *EcoLaw: Legality, Life, and the Normativity of Nature*. London: Routledge.

Del Boca, Angelo. 1992. *Gli italiani in Africa Orientale. Dall'unità alla marcia su Roma*. Rome: Mondadori.

Di Feliciantonio, Cesare and Silvia Aru. 2018. Dai commons al commoning (urbano): pratiche e orizzonti politici nel contesto mediterraneo. Introduzione al numero speciale. *ACME: An International Journal for Critical Geographies* 17(2): 258–268.

Eizenberg, Efrat. 2012. Actually Existing Commons: Three Moments of Space of Community Gardens in New York City. *Antipode* 44(3): 764–782.

Forgacs, David. 2014. *Italy's Margins: Social Exclusion and Nation Formation since 1861*. Cambridge, MA: Cambridge University Press.

Foster, Sheila R. 2019. Urban Commons, Property, and the Right to the City. In *Property Rights from Below*. Routledge.

Foucault, Michel. 1969. *L'archéologie du savoir*. Paris: Gallimard.

Franchetti, Leopoldo. 1985. *Condizioni politiche e amministrative della Sicilia*. Bari: Laterza.

Fraser, Nancy. 2013a. How Feminism Became Capitalism's Handmaiden – and How to Reclaim It. *The Guardian*, 14 October 2013.

Fraser, Nancy. 2013b. *Fortunes of Feminism: From State-Managed Capitalism to Neoliberal Crisis*. London and New York: Verso Books.

Gibson, Mary. 1998. Biology or Environment? Race and Southern "Deviancy" in the Writings of Italian Criminologists, 1880–1920. In *Italy's 'Southern Question'. Orientalism in One Country*, edited by Jane Schneider. London: Routledge.

Ginsborg, Paul. 1990. *A History of Contemporary Italy: 1943–1980*. London: Penguin.

Giglioli, Ilaria. 2017. Producing Sicily as Europe: Migration, Colonialism and the Making of the Mediterranean Border between Italy and Tunisia. *Geopolitics* 22(2): 407–428.

Giorgi, Chiara, ed. 2022. *Welfare. Attualità e prospettive*. Rome: Carocci.

Grabham, Emily. 2016. *Brewing Legal Times: Things, Form, and the Enactment of Law*. Toronto, ON Buffalo, NY and London: University of Toronto Press.

Gramsci, Antonio. 1977. *Quaderni del carcere*. Turin: Einaudi.

Grear, Anna. 2015. Deconstructing Anthropos: A Critical Legal Reflection on "Anthropocentric" Law and Anthropocene "Humanity". *Law and Critique* 26(3): 225–249.

Grimonprez, Benoît. 2022. Les biens communs aux portes du code civil. *Revue de droit rural* 499(1).

Harvey, David. 2008. The Right to the City. *New Left Review* (53): 23–40.

Lefebvre, Henri. 1968. *Le droit à la ville*. Paris: Éditions Anthropos.

Lombardi-Diop, Cristina. 2023. Postcolonial Studies under Erasure: The Politics of the Transnational in Italian Studies. *Forum Italicum* 57(2): 306–314.

Marella, Maria Rosaria. 2013a. 'Pratiche del comune: per una nuova idea di cittadinanza'. *Lettera Internazionale* 116(2): 24–29.

Marella, Maria Rosaria. 2013b. 'La funzione sociale oltre la proprietà'. *Rivista critica di diritto privato* XXXI(4): 551–568.

Marella, Maria Rosaria. 2016. Lo spazio urbano e il diritto del comune. *EuroNomade* (blog). 12 May 2016.

Marella, Maria Rosaria. 2017. The Commons as a Legal Concept. *Law and Critique* 28(1): 61–86.

Mattei, Ugo and Alessandra Quarta. 2015. Right to the City or Urban Commoning? Thoughts on the Generative Transformation of Property Law. *Italian Law Journal* 303(1): 303–325.

Mazzacane, Aldo. 2006. *Oltremare: diritto e istituzioni dal colonialismo all'età postcoloniale*. CUEN.

Minichiello, Giuliano. 1997. *Meridionalismo*. Milan: Bibliografica.

Muehlebach, Andrea. 2012. *The Moral Neoliberal: Welfare and Citizenship in Italy*. Chicago, IL: The University of Chicago Press.

Napoli, Paolo. 2023. Variazioni sull'adagio: la natura può fare a meno dell'uomo. *Filosofia politica* (3): 447–464.

Napoli, Paolo. 2024. Il diritto romano fuori da sé. Yan Thomas e le scienze sociali. In *In ricordo di Yan Thomas*. Pesaro: Intra.

Niceforo, Alfredo. 2012. *L'Italia barbara contemporanea*. Florence: Nabu Press.

Ong, Aihwa. 2006. *Neoliberalism as Exception. Mutations in Citizenship and Sovereignty*. Durham, NC: Duke University Press.

Patriarca, Silvana. 1998. How Many Italies? Representing the South in Official Statistics. In *Italy's 'Southern Question'. Orientalism in One Country*, edited by Jane Schneider, pp. 77–97. Oxford and New York: Berg.

Petersmann, Marie-Catherine. 2023. Life Beyond the Law – From the "Living Constitution" to the "Constitution of the Living". *Zeitschrift Für Ausländisches Öffentliches Recht und Völkerrecht/Heidelberg Journal of International Law* 82(4): 769–800.

Polizzi, Goffredo. 2022. *Reimagining the Italian South: Migration, Translation and Subjectivity in Contemporary Italian Literature and Cinema*. Liverpool: Liverpool University Press.

Portelli, Alessandro. 2009. Un lavoro di relazione. Osservazioni sulla storia orale. www.memoteca.it/upload/dl/E- Book/Alessandro_Portelli.pdf.

Putnam, Robert D. 1994. *Making Democracy Work: Civic Traditions in Modern Italy*. Princeton, NJ: Princeton University Press.

RiverOfLife, Martuwarra, Alessandro Pelizzon, Anne Poelina, Afshin Akhtar-Khavari, Cristy Clark, Sarah Laborde, Elizabeth Macpherson, Katie O'Bryan, Erin O'Donnell and John Page. 2021. Yoongoorrookoo: The Emergence of Ancestral Personhood. *Griffith Law Review* 30(3): 505–529.

Rizzini Ansari, Moniza and Carolina Amadeo. 2022. Law, the City and the Poor: A Roadmap. *City* 26(5–6): 911–928.

Rodotà, Stefano. 1960. Note critiche in tema di proprietà. *Rivista trimestrale di diritto e procedura civile*, 1252.

Rodotà, Stefano. 1974. *Il controllo sociale delle attività private*. Bologna: Il Mulino.

Rositi, Franco. 1993. Strutture di senso e strutture di dati. *Rassegna italiana di sociologia* XXXIV(2): 177–200.

Rossi, Ugo. 2019. Il metodo di Gramsci. Ascesa nazional-populista e nuova questione meridionale in Italia. *Rivista Geografica Italiana* 4: 222–227.
Sauvêtre, Pierre. 2016. Les politiques du commun dans l'Europe du Sud (Grèce, Italie, Espagne). Pratiques citoyennes et restructuration du champ politique. *Actuel Marx* 1 (59): 123–138.
Spanò, Michele. 2013. Istituire i beni comuni. Una prospettiva filosofico-giuridica. *Politica e società* 3: 427–448.
Spanò, Michele. 2015. Le parole e le cose (del diritto). In *Il valore delle cose*, by Yan Thomas, edited by Michele Spanò, pp. 85–98. Macerata: Quodlibet.
Spanò, Michele. 2022. *Fare il molteplice: il diritto privato alla prova del comune*. Turin: Rosenberg & Sellier.
Srivastava, Neelam. 2018. *Italian Colonialism and Resistances to Empire, 1930–1970*. London: Palgrave Macmillan.
Thomas, Yan. 1978. Le droit entre les mots et les choses. Rhétorique et jurisprudence à Rome. *Archives de philosophie du droit* 23: 93–114.
Thomas, Yan. 2002. La valeur des choses. Le droit romain hors la religion. *Annales. Histoire, Sciences Sociales* 57(6): 1431–1462.
Tulumello, Simone. 2016. Reconsidering Neoliberal Urban Planning in Times of Crisis: Urban Regeneration Policy in a "Dense" Space in Lisbon. *Urban Geography* 37(1): 117–140.
Valli, Chiara. 2015. When Cultural Workers Become an Urban Social Movement: Political Subjectification and Alternative Cultural Production in the Macao Movement, Milan. *Environment and Planning A: Economy and Space* 47 (3): 643–659.
Valverde, Mariana. 2015. *Chronotopes of Law: Jurisdiction, Scale and Governance*. New York: Routledge.
Varriale, Andrea. 2015. The Usage of Public Space in Naples – Informality in the Time of Commons. In *RC21 International Conference*. Urbino.
Vercellone, Antonio. 2020. The Italian Experience of the Commons. Right to the City, Private Property, Fundamental Rights. *The Cardozo Electronic Law Bulletin* (1): 1–39.
Vismann, Cornelia. 2008. *Files: Law and Media Technology*. Translated by Geoffrey Winthrop-Young. Stanford, CA: Stanford University Press.

Legal sources

Italian Court of Cassation. 2011. 'Cass., sez. un., 16 febbraio 2011, n. 3813 sull'accertamento della demanialità marittima delle valli da pesca nella laguna veneta'.
Rodotà Commission Bill. 2007. Relazione per la modifica delle norme del codice civile in materia di beni pubblici. In *Atti parlamentari n. 2031*.
Tribunale di Roma. 2012. Ruling of 8/2/2012 on the occupation of Cinema Palazzo.

Chapter 1

The mobilisations for the commons in Palermo in the 2010s

Introduction

Two perpendicular arteries run through the historic centre of Palermo, dividing it into four quarters or *mandamenti*. One axis is Corso Vittorio Emanuele, called "Cassaro" in the Middle Ages and then renamed after the King of Piedmont, which crosses the centre from east to west. The other one is Via Maqueda, named after the Spanish viceroy who ruled Palermo in the seventeenth century. Corso Vittorio Emanuele and Via Maqueda meet at the intersection of the *Quattro Canti* (Four Corners), whose sumptuous buildings represent the four seasons, the four Spanish kings and the four patron saints of the city. Each guards one of the *mandamenti*, or administrative districts, formed by the intersection of the two axes. Kalsa, Il Capo, Ballarò (part of the larger Albergheria) and Borgo Vecchio are areas defined by the presence of historic markets and included in each of the *mandamenti* (Schneider and Schneider 2003: 6).

This chapter examines the movement for the commons in Southern Italian cities in the 2010s focusing on the mobilisations that took place in Palermo, Sicily, at this time. References to the city's social and political events will offer a contextualisation of these practices within the modern history of the Italian South. I begin by focusing on some cultural spaces that were reclaimed as commons and on how such claims inscribed in a national movement for *beni comuni* and a larger trajectory of anti-austerity protests in post-2008 crisis Italy. I then look at grassroots urban regeneration practices that were carried out in the public space by citizens' committees and groups linked to the anti-mafia movement and how, in these cases, the commons were reclaimed as a civic experience empowering local civil society. I focus on legality and participation as the main discourses that informed these practices and on how they played an important role in shaping the government of Southern Italian cities in the recent decades and the post-crisis period. I show how these discursive orders can be contextualised in a specific stage of late capitalist transformation and to what extent they contribute to strengthening a new subjectivity, an "active citizen" whose role is to support an ailing welfare state through volunteer work

DOI: 10.4324/9781003335320-2

(Muehlebach 2012). I examine how the discourses of legality and participation are turned into legal technique through the use of administrative law instruments, and thus transformed into governmental tools, and how this is done by adopting of a top-down, governmental legal notion of the commons. Finally, I focus on the political society as the realm of individuals excluded from the parameters of civil society and on how they renegotiated legality and participation in a materialist and class-conscious perspective by mobilising a radical idea of *beni comuni*. I also focus on the market as the space in which the commons and rights are claimed by the political society and the property interests of the city's marginalised are protected.

Culture as a commons

The Garibaldi Theatre: a manifesto for Palermo's commons

If a symbolic date were to be found to mark the beginning of the mobilisation for the commons in Palermo, it would be 13 April 2012, when the old building of the Garibaldi Theatre was occupied. Known in Palermo simply as *Il Garibaldi*, the theatre has long played a unique role in the city's public imaginary. Built in 1861 in the Kalsa district, the magnificent neoclassical palace was inaugurated with a speech given by one of the main figures of the Italian Risorgimento, Giuseppe Garibaldi. After the Second World War, the building gradually fell into ruin, part of a broader decline affecting the historic centre which was heavily bombed by the Anglo-American Allies in 1943. After reopening in the 1990s, it was closed in 2007 for restoration. It was made accessible again in 2010, only to be closed shortly after, owing to the public administration's doubts about its safety. After years of neglect, in 2012, a group of around sixty artists and precarious cultural workers occupied the theatre and proclaimed it *Teatro Garibaldi aperto* (open Garibaldi Theatre). The political manifesto of the group resonated deeply with the demands of the movement for the commons, which was gaining political momentum across the country at the time:

> Today, we are starting a new project based on the allocation and management of spaces and the creation of a model that will put the city's productive and cultural realities back into circulation, regardless of party interference, patronage blackmail and lack of funding.
>
> We call on the city council of Palermo and other public bodies to publish and make available a census of the spaces they own, to adopt a regulation disciplining their allocation and the economic resources devoted to culture to ensure constant monitoring of all funded activities.
>
> This regulation must be drafted and shared by artists, cultural workers and public officials.

> Only on the basis of a new system of rules can innovative management government models be imagined that finally recognise the identity of all the genders, languages and new histories of this city.

The declaration was significant in several ways. First, through it the occupiers asserted their autonomy from other political and administrative forces in the city. They saw this as a precondition for the self-government of the theatre, which would allow the redistribution of the value generated by it to the artists and the cultural workers that produced it. Second, they denounced that the list of public buildings was not made public and how this omission gave the municipality a hegemonic position in establishing how to manage the spaces. What they proposed instead was to carry out a census of public property and to distribute its control among all the subjects bearing any kind of property interest in it. Third, they asked the municipality to open a debate aimed at creating a new model for the government of public spaces, one determined neither by state nor by market logics – *né pubblico né privato*, as the slogan of the national movement for the commons went.

After the publication of this manifesto, the group occupying the theatre gradually consolidated itself into a collective political subject. This was done through a method, public assembly, as the chosen means of decision-making, similarly to the case of the Valle Theatre in Rome and other occupied cultural spaces in the country. The public assembly was held regularly and was not simply a context for discussing the artistic and cultural activities taking place in the occupied theatre. Above all, these were moments of political debate on how to extend the struggle to other spaces, to occupy and self-govern them. During the assemblies, activists discussed the impact of austerity policies, adopted both nationally and locally under the pressure of budgetary constraints in the post-crisis phase, on several dimensions of collective life, such as the access to culture, education and fundamental rights. The most frequent slogans emerging from these public meetings were *Garibaldi bene comune* ("Garibaldi [as] commons") and *identità bastarde* ("mixed identities").

The occupied Garibaldi Theatre became part of a broad network uniting several occupied cultural spaces in Italy at a time when the national movement for the commons was at its height. The theatre's community considered the possibility of gaining legal status by creating a foundation under private law, following the example of the Valle Theatre. However, the occupation and self-government of the space came to an end in 2014, before any legal status could be acquired by the group. Then, in 2017, the theatre was reopened by public authorities and became the headquarters of Manifesta, the prestigious European Biennal of Contemporary Art, attracting streams of visitors to a historic centre that, as will be explained, underwent a profound socio-economic transformation in the following years, as the tourism industry rapidly expanded in the city.

The Occupied Mediterranean Theatre: a space for the precarious

Another cultural space that was reclaimed as a commons in Palermo in the 2010s was the Teatro Mediterraneo Occupato (Occupied Mediterranean Theatre, or TMO). This occupation concerned the spaces of the Fiera del Mediterraneo, an area located on the slopes of Mount Pellegrino that hosted an important exhibition centre in the post-war period. The pavilions of the fair, owned by the state, were a space for cultural and social exchange for the city and beyond. At the end of 2013, a year and a half after the start of the Garibaldi's occupation, a group of artists and cultural workers in precarious working conditions occupied one of the pavilions. They claimed to act as an open community dedicated to the political project of self-governing a space for social and cultural production. As in the case of the Garibaldi Theatre, they adopted the method of public assembly, with decisions taken by consensus and concerning the planning of activities, the use and transformation of the space and the definition of the principles regulating the artistic production. The declared aim was to experiment with democratic practices and co-operative modes of production and to re-imagine culture beyond consumption – as a commons to be protected from privatisation. To sustain its activities and guarantee an income to artists and cultural workers, the group of occupants resorted to self-financing, donations and exhibitions open to the public.

During the occupation, the relations between the TMO community and the municipality were at times tense and marked by several police eviction attempts. In these circumstances, the occupiers claimed to pursue a radical cultural policy that, unlike that of the municipality, took into account the existence and needs not only of the art and cultural workers but also of the most marginalised residents. When interviewing some of the occupants, I was immediately introduced to a cleavage that would later recur in several conversations during my fieldwork. As one of TMO's first occupants and a long-time activist in the city's radical left scene told me:

> Here we have Libera, Addiopizzo, many anti-mafia associations, and the municipality relies on them. However, we claim the right to act in the same space as these forces. We do not surrender to institutional power, either financially or ideologically.

Implicit in this statement was the perception of a divide between different spheres of activism, one closer to the public actor and the other less embedded in formal power structures. It was during this conversation that I first realised how the groups reclaiming spaces in the city drew on a vocabulary that was widespread in the country's radical politics of the time – that of commons, self-government, autonomous cultural production – to pursue different visions of society.

The mobilisations for the commons in Palermo and elsewhere in Italy in the 2010s were inscribed in a broader trajectory of capitalist transformations and anti-austerity activism. It is useful, in order words, to contextualise them in a local history of socioeconomic change (Tilly 1978). As the same activist told me:

> The initiators of the Wave were students living in precariousness. At some point, we could no longer afford the university fees and the high rents. So it was a revolt, but not like in the seventies. Then you had workers who wanted to liberate themselves. Now it is different. Since 2008, our lives have been precarious not only economically, but also in terms of interpersonal relations and towards institutions. Since 2008, our precariousness is total.

The group occupying the TMO claimed to act on a political continuum with a wide national protest that took place in 2008 called *l'Onda* (the Wave). Back then, the protesters were opposed to the centre-right coalition government led by Silvio Berlusconi, which was considered responsible for pursuing a systematic deterioration of public services through budget cuts particularly affecting public education.[1] In what can be considered as the first stage of anti-austerity mobilisations in the country, the subjectivity animating them was a young, educated class in conditions of partial or total unemployment or employment without social protection – an increasingly precarious population that distrusted both the state and the market (Standing 2011; Della Porta 2015). This protest was inscribed in a supranational dynamic, that of the public sector cuts and weakening of labour protection adopted across Southern Europe after the 2008 crisis (Armingeon and Baccaro 2012).[2]

The cultural warehouses: from the public to the common (and back)

The Garibaldi Theatre and the Occupied Mediterranean Theatre were not the only cultural spaces reclaimed as commons in Palermo in the 2010s. Another case was that of the Cantieri Culturali (Cultural Warehouses, or CC) located in the Zisa neighbourhood. This residential area in the north of the city is named after an Arab-Norman castle built in the twelfth century outside the

1 In 2008 the Berlusconi government passed two laws (133/2008 and 169/2008) that drastically reduced funding for public universities. Protesters claimed that these measures violated the provisions guaranteeing the right to education set out in Articles 33 and 34 of the Italian Constitution.

2 Southern Italy was hit harder by the financial crisis than Northern Italy. After 2008, a widening of the north-south economic divide in the country was reported. Between 2007 and 2009, the national GDP fell by 4.9 per cent, while in Southern Italy it fell by 5.7 per cent. Between 2008 and 2010 the employment rate contracted by 1.5 per cent in Northern and Central Italy and by 4.3 per cent in Southern Italy (Svimez 2011). In 2022 one in three Sicilian households lived in conditions of relative poverty (Istituto Nazionale di Statistica 2023).

ancient walls of Palermo. The CC are a former industrial site including more than twenty warehouses and spreading on a total of about fifty square metres. Their fame is tied to the economic importance they had between the nineteenth and the twentieth century, when they were used as construction sites for building Art Nouveau furniture for ships and palaces.

The dispute over the government of the CC began in the mid-1990s when the city council turned them into a public space for artistic and cultural production. As part of a wider urban regeneration project, twelve of the buildings were earmarked for cultural activities. In the following decade, however, the council shelved the project, a decision which led to the abandonment of the area to a state of industrial archaeology. Years later, in 2011, the municipality published a call for private entities interested in managing the CC, inviting them to submit proposals to cover the restoration costs. Shortly after the call was published, a group of activists and artists occupied the CC under the slogan *cultura bene comune* (culture as a commons). As in the case of the Garibaldi and the TMO, they chose public assembly as method of decision-making and began organising meetings to discuss how the space could be self-governed, also involving the residents.

In 2012, with the end of the right-wing municipal government, the occupation of the CC gained political momentum and became the core of the city's non-institutional politics. As Chiara Giubilaro's research at the time of the occupation shows, the relationship between the occupiers and the municipality was complex and involved a process of negotiation over issues such as access, surveillance and opening and closing hours. Furthermore, a self-branding tactic was pursued by the activists, consisting of the use of marketing techniques to gain visibility in the media and public debate, with actions such as flash mobs and the distribution of leaflets, slogans and logos in the city (Giubilaro 2017: 11). As in the case of the Garibaldi, the occupation faded before the community could gain legal status. In May 2012, when Leoluca Orlando was elected as mayor, the city council started to situate the renovation of the CC within a broader vision, namely the urban renewal that would lead to Palermo's candidacy for European Capital of Culture in 2019. This project implied the transformation of the CC into an important publicly managed venue for the city's cultural policy and was sealed by the appointment of one of the occupants as a municipal advisor in charge of the site's management (ibid.: 18).

Urban regeneration against the mafia

Historical background: the plunder of Palermo

Alongside the reclaiming of cultural spaces as commons, public spaces such as parks and squares in Palermo were also the subject of grassroots claims in the name of *beni comuni*. These practices cannot be fully grasped without considering the peculiar trajectory of the city's urbanisation and the social forces acting behind it, among which, as I will explain, the anti-mafia movement played a prominent role. A helpful starting point for understanding this process is an event dating back to the middle of the twentieth century, the so-called *sacco* (plunder) of Palermo. The historic centre had reached a state of extreme neglect after the Allies' bombing raids forced some 150,000 people to settle in shanty towns and caves, while damaged palaces were abandoned and looted. Jane and Peter Schneider thoroughly reconstructed how the building boom of the 1950s and 1960s revolutionised the city's socio-economic and political outlook for decades to come. From a spatial point of view, the boom consisted of the absorption of the old boroughs in a gigantic urban sprawl extending towards several areas adjacent to the centre. This process destroyed the most of green spaces, tenements and Liberty villas, replacing them with tonnes of concrete. The result was a dramatic architectural and urban reconfiguration, with the city expanding outwards while the historic area, still devastated by bombings, was left to a slow decay. The annihilation of the old city was completed by the construction of the "new Palermo", extending to the north, south and west of the centre into the vast plain called Conca d'Oro (Golden Shell) (Schneider and Schneider 2003).[3] There are several reasons why the plunder of Palermo can be considered one of the most damaging modernist projects ever implemented in a Western city. The first is the context of almost total lack of regulation in which the transformation occurred. Works were largely carried

3 In 1992 a detailed executive plan for the historic centre of Palermo (*Piano particolareggiato esecutivo del centro storico di Palermo*), also known as the Cervellati Plan (*Piano Cervellati*) came into in force, named after the planner Pier Luigi Cervellati, who had already been in charge of the urban redevelopment of Bologna. Handing over the planning to outsiders seemed to be the most appropriate step for the municipality at a historical moment like the early 1990s, when the civil reaction against the mafia was growing strong. Cervellati wanted to prioritise the preservation of existing buildings and public spaces to undo the effects of the previous 1962 plan, which had created the preconditions for the sacco. In the planner's mind, the reconstruction had to philologically reproduce what appeared on maps and land registries of the 1870s and follow a logic of conservation of the existing buildings. The idea, strongly supported by the public administration, was to spatially represent a temporal break: the post-war construction period was a mistake that had to be undone through urban planning. However, the Cervellati plan envisaged some major interventions, such as the complete waterfront renovation, to be pedestrianised before the United Nations Convention on Organized Crime in 1993. The plan aimed to achieve a "soft gentrification" allowing the lower-middle class to repopulate the historic centre (Schneider and Schneider 2003). It was criticised for several reasons, one of the main objections being that it did not match the city's class structure. The initial version of the plan was tailored to Bologna, characterised by the presence of a middle class of craftsmen and professionals. In Palermo, on the other hand, the class structure was more polarised and the middle class narrower. Doubts were also raised on the planners' intention to halt all construction processes. This would have affected Palermo's building sector, a long-standing source of employment and vital part of the city's economy, which would have meant further exposing the lower and middle classes to unemployment and poverty (ibid.).

out by private speculators who made money through rigged tenders and with the involvement of the mafia. Secondly, the effect of the land reform and the agricultural mechanisation in the 1950s and 1960s was to push masses of exploitable peasants into the city. Thirdly, the Christian Democratic political elite, which was in power at the time, created an enormous number of administrative jobs to secure future electoral support. As a result of these elements, Palermo's population grew from 503,000 in 1951 to 709,000 thirty years later, in 1981 (Schneider and Schneider 2003; Dino 2005).

Saving green areas from concrete

One of the many reminders of Palermo's plunder is the Uditore district, among the city's most cemented areas, located to the west of the historic centre and developed around the Parco Uditore. The story of the grassroots urban regeneration of this park is useful for introducing civil society as a social force playing a key role in the trajectory of the Southern Italian commons. In 2010 a group of residents decided to set up a committee with the aim of starting a dialogue with the municipality on the government of the only green space in the neighbourhood, the so-called fondo Uditore. With the slogan "subtracting the Golden Shell from concrete", the group urged the administration to turn this public area into a park, following the example of the urban gardens spreading in North American and European cities. After collecting 8,000 signatures, the committee submitted a project to the city planning office proposing to change the area's zoning from a space for public offices to a site for social use. The administration accepted the proposal and the region, the owner of the *fondo*, financed the work to transform the area into a public park, which was inaugurated in 2012. A few years later, in 2014, the committee acquired legal status by creating a social cooperative aiming to "educate citizens to a sense of belonging to the res publica" and to manage the cooperative's resources with "the diligence and devotion of a good paterfamilias". Volunteers of the cooperative worked from morning to night, seven days a week, to organise the activities needed for the self-financing of the park. The promoted model was one of "good governance", "completely self-financed" and that valued "the communal nature" of the park.[4]

Different actors, then, were expressing different social demands and realising diverse political projects by using the same vocabulary, that of *beni comuni*. In the case of Uditore Park, the commons were invoked not to legitimise an occupation or the collective nature of cultural production, as in the previous cases, but to carry out a citizens' initiative taking place based on values of volunteerism and civic culture.

4 The presentation of the cooperative is available on the website of Parco Uditore: www.parcouditore.org/chi-siamo.

The anti-mafia rescuing the Kalsa

The Uditore Park was not the only case in which citizens mobilised to save a public space from neglect and to rescue it from a fate influenced by criminal interests. Another example of this dynamic in Palermo is Piazza Magione, a square in the heart of the Kalsa district. Devastated by bombings, this space was abandoned after the war and used as a rubbish dump for decades. The piazza and the surrounding area are of symbolic importance not only for the city but also for the country's collective imaginary. Giovanni Falcone and Paolo Borsellino, the anti-mafia judges assassinated by Cosa Nostra in 1992, grew up in this neighbourhood. The first time Piazza Magione was the scene of urban regeneration efforts was at the end of the 1980s, during a period of cultural renaissance known as *primavera palermitana* (Palermitan Spring) that followed a phase of urban violence between families linked to Cosa Nostra, a period known as the mafia wars.[5] Nevertheless, the square remained in a state of abandonment until a group, called Mediterraneo Antirazzista, began to be active in the neighbourhood. In 2008, the group started organising football matches in some popular areas of Palermo, and in 2013, it held its first one in Piazza Magione. A political vision underpinned the collective's activities, namely, countering the socio-economic marginalisation affecting the city's poor and the migrants by promoting sport events as a means to access public space. What animated Mediterraneo Antirazzista was also a critique of the dichotomy between centre and periphery, which in Palermo is counterintuitive compared to cities in the global North, as spaces of social and economic exclusion are also spread out in the geographical centre of the city. In 2013 Mediterraneo Antirazzista launched a campaign to create a children's play area in Piazza Magione. The proposal stemmed from public assemblies involving activists and residents, during which the idea of creating such a space emerged as a way to counter the high rate of school drop-out among the children living in the area. The negotiations with the public administration began in 2016 when the activists called for greater urban renewal efforts on the part of the municipality, both in Kalsa and in the Zen neighbourhood. As a result, two public football pitches were inaugurated, one in each district.[6] The municipality was supported by Addiopizzo, one of the city's main anti-mafia associations, founded in 2004 with the aim of freeing businesses from the

5 The term "mafia wars" refers to two conflicts that took place in Sicily between different factions of Cosa Nostra in 1962 and 1981. The second of these resulted in hundreds of murders and ended with the victory of the Corleonesi clan from the town of Corleone over the Palermitans, who had dominated the organisation until then. For a reconstruction of the history of the Sicilian Mafia, see at least Lupo (2004) and Santino (2008).

6 For an ethnography of Zen and a critical analysis of its construction as marginal through policies and public discourses, see Fava (2008).

pressure of mafia extortion.[7] The association succeeded in creating an ever-expanding *pizzo*-free network of economic and commercial activities and in raising awareness among consumers on the importance of buying from sellers who refuse to be subject to racketeering (Partridge 2012; Elsenbroich 2017). In Kalsa and in other areas of the city Addiopizzo also promotes pedagogic activities on *legalità*, a concept combining the enforcement of the rule of law and the respect for public institutions in a single educational project (Addiopizzo 2022).

The discourse of legality

Discourse, knowledge and power

Observing these mobilisations, I started encountering a rhetorical apparatus defining what was legitimate and what was not in the public sphere – a symbolic and narrative structure that I will refer to as a discourse of legality. Local politicians, businessmen, vendors, social workers, the media, activists and any subject who aspired to play a role in the public realm sought respectability by presenting themselves as operating within specific parameters – those of legality. Whether accepted or critically interpreted, legality delimited the scope of public action and influenced the modes through which the commons were reclaimed.

According to Foucault, discourse is a historically contingent social system capable of producing knowledge and meaning. One of its characteristics is the power to produce material effects or "practices that systematically form the object of which they speak" (Foucault 1969: 49). Discourse is a way of organising knowledge that structures social relations, which must conform to the discourse and accept it as a fact. Although discourse presents itself as absolute and sometimes even ahistorical, it is possible to identify the predetermined rules and ideas that underpin its construction. Discourse thus conceived is closely related to both knowledge and power. With regard to the former, Foucault argues, discourse is ultimately about the creation of knowledge through language. Stuart Hall points to three features that stand out in Foucault's notion of discourse. First, it is not a closed system, as it constantly relies on other discourses to affirm itself. Second, it is produced by a variety of actors linked to different institutions but whoever uses it speaks as its owner, and the statements that make it up are in a regular and never accidental relationship with each

7 *Pizzo* is a word in the Sicilian dialect that refers to the protection money businesses pay to Cosa Nostra to be allowed to carry out their economic activities under the threat of physical and economic damage. Historically, this form of extortion was one of the main ways through which the criminal organisation exercised territorial control (Frazzica et al. 2015).

other (Hall 1992: 201–202). Third, discourse is not only related to knowledge – it is also bound to power and the resulting relationship is triadic. It is power, not facts, that validates something as true. Hence, discourse is also an essential means by which power can circulate (ibid.: 204). As Foucault writes

> "we should admit that power produces knowledge [...] that power and knowledge directly imply one another: that there is no power relation without the correlative constitution of a field of knowledge, nor any knowledge that does not presuppose and constitute [...] power relations".
> (Foucault 1980: 27)

Rise and consolidation of the discourse of legality

The consolidation of the discourse of legality has a specific historical trajectory running through the second half of twentieth-century Italy. The phase of social conflict and political violence that spanned the 1970s peaked at the end of the decade and began to subside in the early 1980s (Della Porta and Tarrow 1986; Cornelissen et al. 2012). In the subsequent phase, important socio-economic and political transformations occurred, including a significant reconfiguration of the judiciary power.[8] Judges were provided with the tools of emergency legislation, which allowed them to criminalise not only individuals but also broader contexts (Della Porta 1993; Cozzolino 2019). The principle of formal legality – the idea that public authorities must refer to a law or an equivalent act working as a legal basis for their decisions – became very relevant in public life.

Several episodes from those years are emblematic of this tendency, such as the series of judicial investigations into corruption scandals among political parties called *mani pulite* ("Clean Hands") in 1992, leading to the fall of the Italian First Republic (Sassoon 1995; Guzzini 1995). The 1990s and 2000s saw the consolidation in the Italian public discourse of a rhetoric in which formal legality was strongly associated with and sometimes conflated with democracy. This was deployed, for example, by the left-wing institutional forces which chose support to the judges as a strategy against Berlusconi's power (Bascetta 2013). A crucial episode for the affirmation of the discourse of legality as a criterion of truth for public action occurred precisely in Palermo. The *Maxiprocesso* ("Maxi Trial") against Cosa Nostra took place between 1986 and 1992 and was followed by the civil society's strong reaction to the murders of judges Falcone and Borsellino by the mafia in 1992.[9]

8 On how this reconfiguration implied a transformation of the modalities of the criminal process in Italy, see Nobili (1998) and Colao (2013).

9 This was one of the most critical judicial events in Italian history, made possible by the Rognoni-La Torre law, which introduced the crime of mafia association into the Italian penal code in 1982. There were nearly 500 defendants, and the first-instance trial ended with 19 life sentences, almost all of which were then confirmed by the Court of Cassation (Dino 2005; Mazzenzana 2016).

Digression: on formal legality and substantial legality

At this point, it is worth making a digression on the role of legality as a principle in Western legal thought and in the Italian legal system more specifically. At the core of liberal constitutionalism is the idea that positive law is the most prominent legal source – all activities carried out by public authorities must draw on a written law promulged by a sovereign parliament. From this principle arises the distinction between formal and substantive legality. While the former implies that public authorities have to refer to law or an equivalent act as the basis for their actions, the latter implies a further step, namely, that a whole body of laws has to be in place to limit public powers and avoid the risk of abuse of power (Rescigno 2016). Marx is one of the leading critics of formal legality as he identified among the flaws of the Hegelian state, founded on law's primacy, the tendency to freeze existing power relations and to only protect the interests of the bourgeois class. Although the class divisions of the ancien régime have been formally abolished, Marx argues, the belief in the abstract and general character of law allows the state to ignore inequalities and ensures the smooth functioning of the capitalist order (Marx 1970).

In the twentieth century, liberal constitutionalism changed its trajectory with the Weimar Constitution of 1919. The parliament was no longer composed exclusively of members of the bourgeoisie, and the law was to become an expression of different class interests. The meaning of legality evolved accordingly: law was to be respected as long as it reflected the values enshrined in the supreme legal source, the Constitution. In the Italian context, the emphasis on the constitutional values underpinning the law was particularly pronounced in the 1960s and 1970s. The concept of constitutional legality sums up this tendency to let the values affirmed in the Constitution prevail over the principle of formal legality. In other words, courts tended to place constitutional values, such as the right to a dignified existence, above the need to respect positive law. As part of this, Italian jurisprudence in the 1970s showed tolerance towards occupations linked to housing needs, stating that in such cases, the principle of legality had to give way to the realisation of a constitutionally guaranteed principle of equality (Nivarra 2008; Quarta 2016).

Palermo as legality's world stage

The history of the Sicilian anti-mafia is closely intertwined with the rise of legality as discourse, which was both criticised and embraced by different sides of the movement at different moments. In the first decades of the Italian Republic, from the late 1940s to the 1960s, the fight against Cosa Nostra was an important left-wing political project. The revolts against the mafia involved a significant component of class critique, addressing the social and economic inequalities that allowed the criminal organisation to flourish.[10] Only at the end of the 1970s, a different current began to emerge, a predominantly urban mobilisation with a liberal orientation stressing the need for cultural change and respect for the rule of law as antidotes to the mafia's power. The emerging polarisation between an "old" and a "new" anti-mafia at that historical moment reproduced on a local scale the central political division that ran through global politics during the Cold War. While the "old" movement was part of a class struggle mostly taking place in rural settings and linked to requests of land reform, the "new" anti-mafia was a prominently urban phenomenon bringing forward "a moral and cultural agenda" enacted by "'pure citizens – ideologically disinterested members of 'civil society'" (Schneider and Schneider 2001: 432).

An episode marking a turning point in this direction was the aftermath of the assassination of Carlo Alberto Dalla Chiesa in Palermo in 1982, who had just been appointed as prefect. The Piedmontese general appeared to the national elite as the ideal statesman for leading the fight against organised crime, having contributed to the dismantling of radical left-wing groups in the late 1970s. His murder provoked a strong dissent in the civil society and the adoption of stricter national anti-mafia laws (Renda 1993). Shortly afterwards, a renewed anti-mafia movement began to be evoked by public voices, one that would focus on educating youth about the values of legality and democracy. The renewed movement should be "more ethical than political" and its members pursue "universal values" such as environmental protection and women's rights (Dalla Chiesa 1983).

Meanwhile, a charismatic figure emerged in Palermo's political scene. The Christian Democrat Leoluca Orlando was elected mayor in 1985 after a campaign in which he presented himself as a champion of the city's civil society. He defined the anti-mafia project as "a car with two wheels", one of which is social and cultural change and the other consisting of police and judicial repression, which had to move in the same direction to succeed (Schneider and Schneider 2003: 160). Orlando remained in office until 1990, during the *primavera palermitana* that followed the mafia wars, expressing the intention to break with the old power structures and the dynamics of collusion between politics and the mafia that had preceded his mandate. These were the years of the *Maxiprocesso*, in which the existence

10 Among the many champions of this anti-mafia season, it is worth remembering Danilo Dolci. A sociologist, educator and writer, he led mobilisations to end poverty and socio-economic exclusion in rural Sicily in the 1950s and 1960s. *Inchiesta a Palermo* and *Banditi a Partinico* are emblematic works of his approach between oral history, social investigation and ethnography. See Dolci (2009, 2013). Peppino Impastato, a young communist activist killed by Cosa Nostra, was another representative figure of the leftist struggle against the mafia. For a reconstruction of his story and the history of Sicilian anti-mafia, see Santino (2000).

of the Sicilian mafia as a specific criminal organisation was legally recognised by Italian judges, and its members sentenced. In 1993, after the assassinations of Falcone and Borsellino, Orlando was re-elected and remained in office until 2000. After the dissolution of the Christian Democratic party, he founded *La Rete* ("The Network"), a political force united by a firm stance against the mafia. The grassroots reaction against the resurgence of mafia violence was immense and led to the creation of associations and citizens' committees working for a radical renewal of society. Among them was the *comitato dei lenzuoli* ("committee of sheets"), which staged an iconic public protest by hanging sheets from the windows with messages against the mafia and the *omertà* looming over the city (Schneider and Schneider 1996).

The unfolding of such events made Palermo a highly symbolic stage for legality, not only nationally but also internationally. In 1999, policymakers from around the world came to the city to participate in an international conference entitled "Educating to legality" organised by Civitas, a non-governmental organisation involved in educational projects to combat corruption and crime. The conference opened with a speech at the Teatro Massimo, the city's opera house, by the then-First Lady Hillary Clinton. In this venue, legality was invoked in a highly rhetorical and metaphorical language. After praising Palermo's civil society for its commitment to the fight against the mafia, Clinton described social order as a "three-legged stool" whose pillars are the government, the economy and the civil society itself (Schneider and Schneider 2003: 285). During the conference, Orlando offered his definition of the anti-mafia movement, presenting it as a cultural revolution building a culture of legality based on renewed ethical values (Orlando 2000).[11]

The emergence of the discourse of legality in Palermo thus took place within a broader national and international juncture.[12] Its consolidation was key for strengthening the liberal and institutional component of the anti-mafia, one less sensitive to the patterns of inequality that have allowed the mafia to proliferate and to offer its form of welfare – work in exchange

11 A few months after the conference, in 2000, Palermo received a positive rating from Moody's Investor Service, expressing satisfaction about a cultural change that could finally bear economic fruit (Schneider and Schneider 2003: 285–288).

12 Since the late 2000s, the discourse of legality got ever more present in the national political debate. It was the mainstay of forces promising an alternative to what was described as the corrupt and predatory "partytocracy" of the centre-left and centre-right parties. The party that used a legalist discourse more than any other in this conjuncture was the Five Star Movement (*Movimento 5 Stelle*), founded in 2009 by the comedian Beppe Grillo and the most voted party in the 2018 elections. On the political phenomenon of the Five Star Movement and its discursive strategies, including legality, see Tronconi (2015).

for protection.[13] As will be explained further in the chapter, some mobilisations for the commons can be read as ways to practice an alternative concept of legality, one that goes beyond formal legality and is critical of the socioeconomic imbalances that organised crime exploits.[14]

The discourse of participation

Instituting participation

In 2012, after eleven years of centre-right local government, Orlando was elected mayor for the fourth time and then for a fifth time in 2017. Under the pressure of the socio-economic disruption following the crisis and following the example of other Italian cities, a City Department for Participation (*Assessorato alla partecipazione*) was set up in 2012 to involve citizens in urban government through participatory processes not mediated by traditional intermediaries such as political parties and unions. In Palermo, as in other Italian cities at the time, the *Assessorato* was an institutional response to the deep crisis of legitimacy experienced by traditional bodies of representation across Western democratic systems – a collapse affecting all forms of political mediation predominant in the second half of the twentieth century. In the crisis moment, this condition of "unrepresentability" was deployed by political elites as a premise for the search for new forms of representation (Spanò and Quarta 2017). At the same time, the idea of creating an *Assessorato* reveals the role that municipalities assigned to themselves, that of giving direction and coherence to the diverse grassroots social demands and coalescing them around a political direction impressed on society through institutional means. Another institution set up in Palermo to this end was the Committee of Cultures (*Consulta delle Culture*), created in 2013 as a

13 In mainstream criminology, some scholars argue that for a mafia organisation to emerge, a structural economic change must occur in the absence of state regulation and property rights system. This would create a strong demand for protection, which the mafia fills with an offer of individuals trained to practice violence (Varese 2013). However, the relationship between the mafia and capitalist development seems to be more complex than approaches centred on formal economy suggest. On this point, see Schneider and Schneider (1976).

14 An early warning of the unintended effects of a discourse building on formal legality came from the Sicilian intellectual and writer Leonardo Sciascia. In an article published in the *Corriere della Sera* in 1987, he recalled how formal adherence to anti-mafia values had already been displayed by fascism as a subtle way of exercising discretionary power in the name of public order. Sciascia highlighted the emergence of "anti-mafia professionals" (*professionisti dell'antimafia*) and how, even in a democratic system, when "rhetoric" replaces "critical spirit", the anti-mafia could become an "instrument of power" (Sciascia 1987). The article caused a great deal of controversy, as the author was accused of undermining the credibility of the anti-mafia struggle and of its champions, the judges.

representative body of all the foreign communities living in Palermo. At first composed of twenty-one members, each elected by a different national group in the city, the *Consulta* was conceived as an advisory body to the city council: its recommendations were not binding but provided advice to public officials, similarly to a classic mechanism of representative democracy exercising a form of soft power over the public administration.

Italy's catholicisation of neoliberalism

Alongside legality, participation emerged as another discourse in the Italian public realm in the post-2008 economic crisis conjuncture. In an ethnographic study on the neoliberal transformation of Lombardy's economy and society occurring since the late 1970s, Andrea Muehlebach focuses on the moral dimension of this change, that is, on the "moralised kind of citizenship" that developed during the time of social services privatisation (Muehlebach 2012: 6). The argument is that as the state gradually retreats from its role of leading provider of social services, it mobilises the population into a labour regime based on volunteer work. Ethical citizenship thus emerges as "a new mode of social and moral subjectivity, new assumptions about citizens' rights and duties, and new conceptualisations of human agency, affect, and will". These ideals and policies are then mediated through bureaucratic structures and legal frameworks and take root in society through "state-mediated pedagogical practice". The development of this ethic, peculiar to neoliberal capitalism, updates and thickens Foucault's argument on modernity as a phase in which power passes through the body and no longer through the soul. What is produced is a "soulful" citizenry turning emotions into publicly valuable deeds: statecraft thus becomes soulcraft (ibid.: 17–18).

Critical scholarship has already highlighted how a fundamental element of the ethos of neoliberal capitalism is the state's refusal to take responsibility for citizens' socio-economic safety (Bhandar 2016) and how an entrepreneurialised and individualised social responsibility emerges at its place (Brown 2015). Nevertheless, there seems to be something specific in the flourishing of ethical citizenship in late-capitalist Italy. What is distinctive about the trajectory of Italian capitalism is a unique articulation of Catholic and market values, held together by a loving and empathetic subject whose mission is to mitigate, through individual actions, the damage caused to society by the extension of the market logic to all spheres of life (Muehlebach 2013).[15] The acts of charity performed by this citizen are affective responses that depoliticise solidarity by glossing over the root of inequalities, thus making welfare a private matter (Kaika 2017).

15 Of course, this idea of morality as central to capitalist transformation is consolidated. It recalls Benjamin's reflections on capitalism as a religion (Benjamin 1985), the Weberian argument on the calvinist roots of capitalism (Weber 2010) and Polanyi's thesis that every wave of marketisation is opposed by a counter-movement aimed at defending society from dissolution (Polanyi 1957).

A legal genealogy of participation

It is worth sketching a genealogy of the concept of participation, focusing on its historical and moral foundations as well as on its legal ones. An essential tool for the conceptualisation of participation in the Italian legal framework is National Law 328 of 2000, which established "an integrated system of social interventions and services". This law paved the way for a reform of the Italian welfare system by establishing that, while the state must still guarantee the universality of social rights, it is no longer the main subject in charge of deciding on the provision of social services. Importantly, this law recognised third-sector organisations as legitimate subjects not only for providing services but also for the strategic planning of welfare. It introduced a set of administrative tools named *piani di zona* ("zone plans"), lasting three years and aimed at building a shared welfare system involving citizens in all stages of decision-making at the local level. Some aspects make the zone plans a problematic legal instrument. First, the plans identify only a few third-sector organisations, which are not necessarily representative of the whole population's composition and needs. Second, local communities are presented in the plans as cohesive and homogeneous entities, with no attention to the unequal power relations or potential conflicts within them. Third, the concept of citizen participation is vaguely defined and there is no indication of how it can be enacted in practice. In short, the law is built on normative claims that do not clarify the mechanisms through which participatory processes can be activated from the grassroots. Law 124 of 2015 has further expanded the relevance of citizens' participation in the local structuring of social services and goes in the same direction (Colombo and Gargiulo 2016). The recourse to a generic grammar of participation thus displays its potential to serve as a tool for the bureaucratisation and co-optation of social needs and demands (Kelty 2016). Based on a formal notion of participation, it contributes to the realisation of top-down urban governance models masked as bottom-up processes. A gradual withdrawal of the state from regulatory tasks in the service sector and a significant transfer of responsibilities to private subjects can, indeed, take place under the guise of citizen participation.

The discourse of participation, and the ethical citizen as its agent, was consolidated also at the supranational legal level. The principle of subsidiarity enshrined in the EU legislation has played a crucial role in this sense (Muehlebach 2013).[16] First included in the Maastricht Treaty of 1992 and later in the Treaty on the European Union of 2007, it is formulated as follows:

16 Andrea Muehlebach points to the Catholic matrix of the subsidiarity principle. The Catholic social doctrine – the set of theories and concepts elaborated by the Catholic Church to deal with contemporary social issues – has subsidiarity at its core. According to the doctrine, negating subsidiarity in the name of social equality means to hamper the spirit of freedom and initiative. Pope Benedict XVI argued in 2009 that subsidiarity is the greatest antidote against an omnipresent welfare state. This is a contemporary articulation of a discourse that has long

> Under the principle of subsidiarity, in areas which do not fall within its exclusive competence, the Union shall act only if and in so far as the objectives of the proposed action cannot be sufficiently achieved by the Member States, either at central level or at regional and local level, but can rather, by reason of the scale or effects of the proposed action, be better achieved at Union level.
>
> (Art. 5(3) of the Treaty on the European Union)

The envisaged model is one in which the government's action has to be implemented at a level as close as possible to the local one. If action at this scale is impossible, interventions can take place at a higher level. The concept of subsidiarity was enshrined in the Italian legal system with the constitutional reform of 2001:

> Administrative functions are attributed to the Municipalities, unless they are attributed to the provinces, metropolitan cities and regions or to the State, pursuant to the principles of subsidiarity, differentiation and proportionality, to ensure their uniform implementation.
>
> Municipalities, provinces and metropolitan cities carry out administrative functions of their own as well as the functions assigned to them by State or by regional legislation, according to their respective competences.
>
> […] The State, regions, metropolitan cities, provinces and municipalities shall promote the autonomous initiatives of citizens, both as individuals and as members of associations, relating to activities of general interest, on the basis of the principle of subsidiarity.
>
> (Art. 118 of the Italian Constitution)[17]

From discourse to legal technique

Legality and participation are not just discourses. They have also entered a realm crucial for the government of urban space, namely administrative law. In the 2010s, alongside the notion of the commons introduced by the Rodotà Commission, a legal concept emerged that introduced a governmental vision of *beni comuni*. The legal tool that consolidated this approach is the "Regulation on the collaboration between citizens and administration for the care, regeneration and shared management of urban commons". First adopted in Bologna in 2014, it has since been used in more than three hundred municipalities across the country.[18] This instrument builds a government

been conducted by part of the Catholic Church on the homology between an individual tied to a family and a community and the sacralisation of property as a natural right (Muehlebach 2013).

17 Criticism of the reformed Article 118 regarding its potential to undermine public welfare abounds. See, among others, Lucarelli (2013).

18 The municipalities that adopted the regulation are 312 (as of April 2024).

structure of the commons based on shared administration, that is, an "organisational model which, by implementing the constitutional principle of horizontal subsidiarity, allows citizens and administration to carry out activities of general interest on an equal level". The regulation grants a specific legal status to those who reclaim the commons, that of "active citizens", i.e., "all subjects [...] who, regardless of the requirements concerning residence or citizenship are active for even limited periods of time for the care, regeneration and shared management of common goods pursuant to this regulation". The commons are identified as "goods, both material and immaterial, which citizens and the administration recognise as functional to the well-being of the community and its members, to the exercise of fundamental human rights and the interest of future generations, taking action accordingly towards them pursuant to Article 118 paragraph 4 of the Italian Constitution [...]" (Tonanzi 2020)".

An ad hoc administrative function is thus introduced, which involves grassroots communities and civil servants participating on an equal footing in the goverment of the commons. The latter are recognised as such by the citizens and the administration in a joint effort, so the moment of institutional recognition becomes crucial. A specific administrative function, the Office for the shared administration (*Ufficio per l'amministrazione condivisa*), is set up to evaluate citizens' proposals and qualify spaces as commons. In this model, the legitimate way for individuals and groups to reclaim the commons is to fill in a form and send it to the Office. Activities of commoning include "cleaning, painting small ordinary maintenance, gardening, decorations, activities of territorial animation, social aggregation communication, cultural and educational activities". The regulation also introduced a private law tool to be adopted after the recognition of the commons, called Pact of collaboration, a contract listing objectives and criteria for the inclusion and exclusion of individuals in the management of the commons. A solid educational aspect is at stake, as the municipalities must promote and organise courses addressed to public servants and citizens to strengthen the "culture of collaboration between citizens and administration" also in schools (ibid.).

The main legal basis for such a conceptualisation of the commons is not the fulfillment of the individual's fundamental rights, as in the Rodotà Commission's definition, but rather the principle of subsidiarity. (Angiolini 2016). Another aspect that differs significantly from the Commission's approach is the rigidity of the authorised use of property, which cannot be modified. In the legal formulation of the commons proposed by the Commission, the function (the exercise of rights) is paramount, opening up to a multiplicity of uses that can differ significantly from those originally intended for the public or private spaces reclaimed as commons.

The regulation seems to transpose into law three ideals that have been relentlessly championed by Italian elites as cornerstones of a renovated civic culture in the post-austerity phase: a concept of legality meant as the respect of legal rules and loosely associated with the achievement of social and economic justice; a notion of participation with moralistic features, aimed at mobilising citizens to support state welfare through volunteer work; and *decoro urbano* (urban decorum) as an ideology for ordering urban space along axes of security and sanitisation to make it appealing to visitors and investors (Bukowski 2019; Pecile 2022). Adopting this regulation in hundreds of Italian cities over the past decade has made it possible to transform these values into governmental techniques, affirming the commons as the collective responsibility of a moralised citizen.[19]

The regulation for the shared management of the commons was promoted by Labsus, an association working at the national level to promote the principle of horizontal subsidiarity through projects involving public administrations and local communities. The idea animating the association is that people have "capacities", not just "needs", and that these can be used to solve problems of "common concern" in collaboration with the local instances of government. The government's partner is a citizen willing to offer labour as a volunteer, without receiving any compensation, "while getting deep personal satisfaction".[20]

Negotiations to adopt the regulation in Palermo began in 2017 when members of Labsus declared that using this tool as a legal framework for the city's commons would have been a significant step towards no longer thinking of the city in terms of poverty and inequality, but instead associating it with concepts such as "quality of life" and "solidarity" (Bravetti 2017). The regulation was finally approved in April 2023 in an amended version, modifying the original proposal in some aspects (Comune di Palermo 2023).

The Labsus regulation is emblematic of how a disciplinary vision of urban space can be enacted through a legal concept of the commons based on the subsidiarity principle. The co-existence of radical and conservative uses of the law to reclaim the commons will be examined in the next chapter. For now, it is worth noticing how the regulation – in particular, the concepts of shared administration and ethical citizenship that it contains – validates a concept of civil society as the subject legitimately reclaiming the commons, both morally and legally – or rather legally insofar as morally.

19 Foucault defines government as "the activity that consists in governing people's conduct within the framework of, and using instruments of, a State" (Foucault 2008: 318). It is distinct from governmentality, which he later introduces to refer to both the practice of government and the way of thinking about it – the rationality of government (Gordon 1991). Governmentality is famously defined as "the ensemble formed by institutions, procedures, analyses and reflections, calculations, and tactics that allow the exercise of this very specific, albeit very complex, power that has the population as its target, political economy as its major form of knowledge, and apparatuses of security as its essential technical instrument" (Foucault 2009: 144).

20 With these words the Labsus project is presented on the website of the association: www.labsus.org/chi-siamo.

The critique of civil society developed by Gramsci becomes useful at this point. A form of domination that is not despotic but indirect, based on concessions made by the dominant groups to the dominated to incorporate their demands into the state structure: this is how hegemony is exercised throughout society – as an educational relationship (Gramsci and Hobsbawm 2000; Conelli 2022). Civil society is the realm in which hegemony emerges as the result of an unequal power relationship and in which the interests of the dominant groups eventually appear as everyone's interests.

Of course, since Gramsci wrote about civil society and hegemony, the capitalist system is no longer the same. In neoliberal capitalism, resources and services are managed through market logic while the state still performs certain functions, such as securing property rights (Harvey 2008). The state's ally in this transformation is an entrepreneurial and self-investing subject as a historically specific declination of the *homo oeconomicus* (Brown 2015). Definitions, nouns and words are essential to establish hegemony. In the case of neoliberal hegemony, it is the vocabulary of economics that plays a central role: the keywords are market relations, choice and self-interest, with the acceptance of ever-increasing levels of inequality as a result (Massey 2013). In post-crisis Italy, civil society is a space for this lexicon to circulate; the law is the technique that allows this discourse to be legitimised and inscribed in social and urban space. It is through it that the subjectivity of the active citizen is both named and disciplined – in one word, instituted.

Beyond civil society

Political society and the market space

Having seen how the commons can be legally conceptualised in a governmental way, affirming a civil society based on values of legality and participation, we may ask who remains excluded from this realm. In other words, we may interrogate which society lies outside of civil society in the Italian South, and how the concept of the commons is mobilised in that realm.

The point of departure to address these questions is postcolonial theory and the rethinking of the cleavage between civil society and political society that has been carried out in this literature. Central to Gramsci's thought, this distinction is reinterpreted by Partha Chatterjee, who argues that political society coincides with the vast majority of the world's population, a group incessantly engaged in the production of the "political" – a constellation of diverse social practices that amount to the politics of the governed. Foucault's concept of governmentality is thus reread actively – from the subalterns' perspective. Chatterjee emphasises how the distinction between citizens on one side and population on the other has been crucial to the organisation of Western modern politics: "citizens inhabit the domain of theory, populations the domain of policy" (Chatterjee 2004: 34). While citizens are the ideal moral subject of the modern state, the population is made up of individuals who do not fit into the modern ideals of citizenship, rights and property – all those excluded from the imaginary of modernity (Spanò 2017). The context in which the population exists and acts is political society, where the values orienting public action can differ significantly from those animating civil society.

Chatterjee's reformulation of the distinction between civil and political society provides a useful analytical framework not only for postcolonial settings but also for understanding dynamics specific to Western political life, in particular how modern citizenship has been advancing through processes of exclusion. Political society becomes an essential tool for constructing a critique of capitalist societies from the point of view of the governed (Mezzadra 2007). It is a particularly useful category for the Italian South, which was not the direct object of colonisation but was consistently constructed as the "Other" vis-à-vis the developed North in a national project structured on a North/South divide. As Carmine Conelli writes, "watermarks of colonialism" can be found in the making of the Italian South as the "nation's reverse" (Conelli 2022: 58). The persistence of these watermarks allows for a postcolonial reading of the social and economic dimensions of the Italian South.

Where is political society in a Southern Italian city? In which social and urban space do we find it? We should look at the places where the dynamic that unfolds is what Conelli calls an "alley economy": a set of relations that the bourgeois and middle classes maintain with artisans, pieceworkers, hawkers – a fragmented popular class that lives across the boundaries between formal and informal, legal and illegal work (ibid.: 170-176). While civil society is asked to follow the logic of the rule of law and formal citizenship, the spaces of political society are traversed by negotiations and conflicts handled according to other criteria. New subjectivities are crafted in these tense spaces, inhabited by individuals who are not the recipients of discourses of legality and participation.

One of these spaces is the market, the part of the urban territory designated by the public authorities for buying and selling activities. Explaining the role of European markets in capitalist modernisation, Giacomo Todeschini underlines how the emergence of civil society during the transition to modernity implied the exclusion of large parts of the urban population from public space.[21] A fundamental site in which this process took place is the modern market, a

21 This is the conjuncture in which the poor of the city ceased to be supported by charitable structures of the church and private subjects and became a social issue to be managed through public assistance (Coccoli 2017).

historical form of spatial organisation resulting from a double gesture of identification made by public authorities towards two different groups: the faithful, worthy of trust and of being considered part of society and therefore included; and those who, because of their untrustworthiness – confessional and legal – were branded as infidels and excluded. The market thus sums up the ambiguous character of European modernisation, which, on the one hand, sought to draw the population into a seemingly inclusive space and, on the other, did so according to specific rules establishing cultural, economic and racial hierarchies between groups. In modern societies, inequality first materialised through an unequal distribution of the ability to participate in the market (Todeschini 2007).[22]

The historic market of Ballarò

One of the spaces in which political society can be found in Palermo is the market, particularly the historic one of Ballarò. The neighbourhood stretching between the cathedral and the central railway station has been hosting a large open-air market since the Arab domination in the tenth century. After the war bombings, this area was mainly inhabited by the popular classes and was the place where many foreign communities settled.[23] For decades now, the area has been home to a vibrant network of associations and organisations working for social inclusion, even more so in recent years in the context of the European migration crisis (Wulff Barreiro and Brito Gonzalez 2020). In Ballarò, the ways in which residents inhabit and use space are such that the distinction between the public and the private is blurred. From a legal and governmental perspective, this means that the actual uses of space go beyond what is allowed by law. One of the effects of this is that many properties in the historic centre are not easily tradable, which hinders or slows down gentrification processes (Bartoli 2019).

Besides being home to one of the city's largest open-air markets, since the late 2000s, this area of Palermo has been the location of a flea market that has developed into an informal space of economic exchange, called by the locals *mercato del riuso* ("market of re-use"). Its regulars are individuals who cannot

22 For a *longue durée* historical approach to inequalities reconstructing how they are generated by the recurrence of similar social processes, see Tilly (1998).

23 In their ethnography of the anti-mafia movement in Palermo, Jane and Peter Schneider acknowledged the difficulty of defining the city's less privileged residents in terms of *the* working class. This label would misleadingly indicate white collar, and not blue-collar jobs, and would not account for the reality of a mostly under- or unemployed population, "immersed in very small-scale, often off-the books" kind of activities. They thus propose to speak of "popular classes" (an approximate translation of the Italian expression *il popolo*) or even "working classes", in the plural, to account for "a more open and varied understanding of work" carried out by individuals who often rely on external mediation to obtain services, housing and jobs (Schneider and Schneider 2003: 233).

access the economy through formal channels and exercise their rights in ways that do not correspond to the ideals of modern civil society. The market of re-use has provided a source of modest income for the city's poor in the context of growing urban poverty after the 2008 crisis (ibid.).[24] This is not the site of one legality, but of multiple ones; legalities are "porous", in the sense that the market is crossed by "a network of different day-to-day negotiations with power that renders vacuous any neat binary of legal/illegal" (Liang 2005: 15). Spaces like this, in which diverse legalities co-exist, reveal a conflict that has to do with ideas of property– with the co-existence of clashing property regimes (Cuff 1998). On the one hand, a public property regime exists in the market space, in which the interest of the owner – the public actor – prevails. On the other hand, a common property regime which, although not formalised, competes with the former and has to do with the collective interest of non-owners to use and access the space.

Before delving into how these different property regimes are made and unmade through the interaction between the public actor and activists, it is worth focusing on the transformation that the urban space of Ballarò underwent in the 2010s. Now one of the city's main tourist attractions, parts of the neighbourhood have gone through a process of grassroots urban regeneration since 2011, which only later caught the municipality's attention and inspired its policies. In those years, the socio-economic structure of Ballarò began to change significantly. An increase in the number of middle and upper-class settlers – tourists, but also new residents – was registered, with the appearance of different lifestyles and consumption patterns from those of the locals and of the students who crowded the lively bars at night. A space epitomising the urban regeneration practices conducted by activists in Ballarò is Piazzetta Mediterraneo. A small rectangular square close to the bustling daily market, this space has had a long and turbulent history. Originally a sacred place – the Catholic Church owns it – it was destroyed in the bombing raids of the Second World War. It was then used for decades as an abusive car park and rubbish dump. In 2011 activists from Mediterraneo Antirazzista, together with a collective called *Giardinieri di Santa Rosalia* ("Gardeners of Santa Rosalia", after the patron saint of Palermo), began to clean it up and decorate it with benches, plants and murals. The space was named Piazzetta Mediterraneo and became the regular meeting place for a network of local associations. In 2013 the city council recognised the name of the square and began to implement a policy of urban regeneration in the area. As part of it, in 2015 an agreement was signed with

24 According to the municipality of Palermo, there were 20,000 families in conditions of absolute poverty in the city as of 2017 (Giubilaro 2019). In recent years, ISTAT (the Italian National Statistics Institute) has described a country in which absolute poverty is increasing and disproportionately affects the South (Istituto Nazionale di Statistica 2023).

the Church for a free loan that turned the space into public property for the next twenty years.

Negotiating through law

Ballarò is emblematic of the entanglement of socio-economic marginalisation and touristic transformation that has been affecting a number of cities of the Italian South in recent years. In this neighbourhood, a new political subject emerged in the 2010s that was able to build a grassroots critique of the ongoing social and economic transformations. It was the public assembly of SOS Ballarò, in which the three letters stand for *Storia, Orgoglio, Sostenibilità* ("history, pride, sustainability"). Initially inspired by the aim of building a collective response to a series of mafia intimidations in the area (Montagnani 2020), it was set up by activists coming from different political traditions, ranging from Catholic to left-wing groups.[25] The collective began to assemble to discuss issues affecting the residents' everyday lives, such as the lack of access to public infrastructures, the state of abandonment of several buildings, and the widespread conditions of poverty. In 2015 the first joint public assembly with members of the city council was held and a long negotiation between activists and public authorities began. Gradually, discussions started addressing how the regeneration of Ballarò could be organised from the bottom up, directly involving the residents and focusing on market vendors and migrants, regardless of their legal status. Excluded from formal socio-economic structures, these subjects are an essential presence in a neighbourhood that was becoming one of the city's main tourist sites, owing to its "folkloric" and "authentic" feel. This mobilisation differed from other cases, in which the ideals of civil society oriented public action, because of the direct involvement of the city's political society. SOS Ballarò was born out of a spirit of resistance to two elements: the dominant narrative portraying the area as a place of decay and the marginalisation and displacement of residents accelerated by the touristic transformation of Ballarò (Giubilaro 2019). Activists adopted a method – assembly – based on the residents' participation, especially the migrants and the *mercatari*, the vendors "out of order" with the law. Through the assemblies, they managed to create an informal space to represent them and bring their demands to the city council's attention. SOS Ballarò thus achieved two objectives: to create a counter-narrative about the neighbourhood able to dismiss the stigmatisation targeting its residents, and to seek solutions for the paradoxical situation experienced by people living in Ballarò, at once those generating the

25 The first category included local groups such as ones of the Oratorio Santa Chiara and the Centro Sociale San Saverio, while the second one more recently formed collectives such as Mediterraneo Antirazzista, the Circolo Arci Porco Rosso and the social enterprise Moltivolti.

area's attractiveness through their everyday lives and the last to benefit from the wealth generated by tourism. One of the activists of SOS Ballarò resumed the paradoxical situation of the marginalised residents and the difficulty of designing rules to redistribute the wealth generated by tourism in their favour with these words:

> Tourists now come to Ballarò and take pictures of the vendors because they look folkloric. Then they go somewhere else to eat. This is the problem: the market creates enormous value, but residents, vendors, no one here really benefits from it. The businesses that benefit are outside the market area, not in it. New social classes are hanging around here with their ways of consumption that vendors cannot satisfy. This has already happened in the Vucciria [another historic market in the centre], and the result was the destruction of the market.

The presence of new social classes in Ballarò led to increased police controls, which are disruptive to the alley economy.

> We told the authorities this: increasing police controls in Ballarò is not the solution. All the vendors carry out activities that violate one or another norm, for example, regarding the preservation of food. These practices were tolerated for many years because they were seen as forms of self-organisation. A man used to sell eggs in what is now Piazzetta Mediterraneo for sixty years; these eggs were certainly not "legal", but nobody ever died from eating them.

One of the harshest interventions by public authorities took place in 2019, at the time of this conversation, when spaces in Ballarò were inspected and vendors sanctioned for their activities:

> Everything in Piazzetta Mediterraneo is now closed, seized by the police. We are trying to talk to the police station and the port authority to convince them that the economic activity of the fish traders must be preserved... And we are failing. We have managed to have some exchanges with the municipality, but then there are too many authorities involved in this issue and it is just too difficult. We can do quick fixes, but we cannot solve the problem.

To intervene in this dynamics, SOS Ballarò resorted also, and importantly, to tactic uses of law. Protecting the right of the marginalised residents to use and access public space implied negotiating new rules recognising their property interests as legitimate. Negotiations brought to the adoption of the municipal Regulation 81 of 2017, allocating around three hundred stalls to individuals involved in informal selling activities and qualifying them as "vendors by need" – a definition emphasising the social function of the market, defined in the document as "a concrete response to the condition of extreme poverty of those who sell used goods" (Comune di Palermo 2017a). Later, the approval of Regulation 120 of 2019 strengthened the protection guaranteed to vendors, setting up rules on opening and closing times and a joint control system managed between the police, the municipality and vendors themselves (Comune di Palermo 2019). The establishment of these rules aimed to reconnect the wealth generated in the market with those who produce it. Meanwhile, vendors acquired legal status by creating an association, Sbaratto, allowing them to interact with the public actor from a safe position and through activists' mediation (Montagnani 2020).[26]

At the heart of SOS Ballarò's political project, which guided the adoption of the regulations, was a critical reinterpretation of legality and participation and of what it means to claim a collective right to use and access public space to the benefit of the city's marginalised. Read through a class-conscious vision, legality and participation were re-signified away from their institutional interpretations. Legality was no longer equated with mere compliance with existing legal rules but conceived as a process of reducing poverty and marginalisation, even if this implied challenging the existing norms. As one of the SOS Ballarò activists once told me, legality is desirable when it is helpful to the marginalised – when it allows them to pay less taxes, build their businesses and secure their lives. Practicing legality in this way means intervening on the roots of the socio-economic inequality that increased after the crisis.

Even participation was radically reconceived away from its predominant meaning. Rather than a normalising discourse validating the participation of certain citizens in neoliberal modes of urban governance (Roura-Expósito and González 2018), it became a critical tool to rebalance the interactions among subjects crossing urban space from different power positions expressed by diverse property interests. Participation was thus reinvented as an everyday practice conducted through assemblies in which asymmetrical power relations and property interests were challenged.

Reclaiming the commons for political society

Welfare from below: Anomalia's self-governed medical clinic

Other cases of commons reclaimed beyond the parameters of civil society developed in Palermo in the 2010s. Some of these were directly related to asserting social rights, such as the right to health, in the context of their erosion

26 The legal point of reference for the negotiations was the *Regolamento Unico dei Mercati*, ("Single Regulation of Markets"), adopted by the City Council in 2016 and aimed at improving the conditions of the historic markets in the city centre.

and privatisation. In 2016 a self-governed medical clinic was set up in the occupied space of Anomalia in the popular area of Borgo Vecchio. Located near the nineteenth-century Ucciardone prison building, Anomalia is emblematic of a type of urban mobilisation that has been taking place in Italy since the late 1970s. *Centri sociali* are self-governed structures created after a group occupies an abandoned public or private property. Their political connotation is strong: often close to counterculture, members identify mainly with radical left-wing or anarchist positions (Andretta 2005; Montagna 2006). The identity of each *centro sociale* combines an international component – of solidarity within a network of groups and global political causes – with a local element tied to offering services and spaces to residents and providing the conditions for communal living. *Centri sociali* have a strong relationship with the areas in which they are rooted and observing them is useful for examining the impact of urban policies at a local scale (Gargiulo and Cirulli 2006).

After decades of experimenting with self-government, activists of the *centri sociali* crossed paths with the movement for the commons. The story of Anomalia is an example of this encounter and what it could bring. In 2012, activists from the Wave mobilisation occupied an abandoned public building and turned it into a *centro sociale*. When I visited it, the space was organised in this way: a popular gym accessible to residents, a bar and, later, a self-organised medical clinic. Activists organised public leisure events, such as concerts and film screenings, as well as open assemblies and debates on issues affecting the neighbourhood.

The medical clinic was founded to provide healthcare to the residents of Borgo Vecchio living in conditions of social and economic marginalisation. Against public healthcare erosion, activists conceived the clinic as a neither public nor private structure for the fulfilment of the right to health. The residents of Borgo Vecchio were experiencing restricted access to public structures despite the neighbourhood's relatively central location – the wealthy area of Via Libertà is only a few hundred metres away. The clinic was open six days a week, thanks to the volunteer work of around twenty doctors, some of whom retired, and with the support of a private laboratory for medical examinations. Services included specialist consultations (such as cardiology, gynaecology and neurology) and generalist appointments; medical equipment was purchased through crowdfunding and public donations. According to the involved activists, most of the clinic's patients were people living in poverty, including individuals coming from other neighbourhoods and irregular migrants who were not allowed to access public healthcare, owing to their lack of legal status (Pecile 2017).

Alongside the clinic visits, Anomalia offered a series of socio-medical activities to raise awareness on disease prevention, focusing on illnesses that carry social stigma, such as hepatitis A. The idea was to mobilise the population to reclaim and reappropriate the right to health as a commons, outside private and public structures, and to imagine a grassroots form of welfare. The political project of the self-organised medical clinic in Anomalia thus combined two dimensions. In addition to compensating for the erosion of public services in a context of economic recession, it contributed to rooting practices of self-government and solidarity in the neighbourhood based on the reclaiming of health as a commons. This experience was in continuity with similar initiatives across Southern European cities in the era of austerity, when non-state forms of welfare began to be experimented with, and solidarity was affirmed over participation as a principle for collective action (Cabot 2016; Arampatzi 2017).

Experimenting with civic uses: Theatre Montevergini as a commons

Another case of the commons being reclaimed beyond civil society in Palermo is that of the Montevergini Theatre. Located in the historic area of the Capo, this fifteenth-century public building was occupied in 2016 after years of abandonment. A group of artists and precarious cultural workers began to take care of it, explicitly referring to the commons as a mode of self-government. In their open letter to the city, which served as their manifesto, they declared to be inspired by ideals of social co-operation, mutualism, sharing of time and knowledge, and building interdependence between members as an expression of direct democracy and care for the commons. Occupants defined themselves as part of the Italian struggle for *beni comuni* and close to the reclaiming of the ex-Asilo Filangieri as a commons in Naples, where activists revived the institution of civic use to guarantee the collective use and access to the space, as will be explained in Chapter 4. With the approval of Council Resolution 74 of 2017, establishing the civic and collective urban use model at the Montevergini Theatre, the municipality provided the space with the legal status of commons. The Neapolitan experience was cited as a virtuous example of how urban civic and collective use can be used as a new institution for direct self-government of spaces. The resolution cites two legal sources as the basis for recognising Montevergini as a commons. The first is Article 43 of the Constitution, which provides that law may establish that a community of users controls public services for the purposes of the common good. In this way, it is recognised that the right to education and to a dignified existence is fulfilled by governing the theatre as a commons. Secondly, the regulation mentions Law 1766 of 1927 on the civic use of pastures, forests and agricultural land as its legal basis (Comune di Palermo 2017b).

Compared to the Labsus regulation, this legal instrument shows a progressive use of law. Not only are the commons freed from any connection to the subsidiarity principle and strongly associated with the exercise of fundamental rights, thus liberating the community from a moral and governmental duty towards public space. What is recognised is also the distinction between the property title and the function of the space, linked to its use, as a tactic to enact the commons in the existing legal system. However, the lack of consistent actions from the municipality's side contributed to the end of the political experience of Montevergini (Micciarelli 2021). As will be explained in Chapter 3, other legal instruments – belonging to both private and public law – can be used to enact the commons as a counter-hegemonic form of property.

References

Addiopizzo. 2022. Progetto Scuola. https://addiopizzo.org/project/progetto-scuola.

Andretta, M. 2005. Movimenti e democrazia tra globale e locale: il caso di Napoli. In *La democrazia locale tra rappresentanza e partecipazione*, F. Gelli (Ed.). Milan: Franco Angeli, pp. 281–318.

Angiolini, Chiara. 2016. Possibilità e limiti dei recenti regolamenti comunali in materia di beni comuni. In *Beni comuni 2.0. Contro-egemonia e nuove stituzioni*, Alessandra Quarta and Michele Spanò (Eds). Milan-Udine: Mimesis, pp. 147–156.

Arampatzi, Athina. 2017. The Spatiality of Counter-Austerity Politics in Athens, Greece: Emergent "Urban Solidarity Spaces". *Urban Studies* 54(9): 2155–2171.

Armingeon, Klaus and Lucio Baccaro. 2012. Political Economy of the Sovereign Debt Crisis: The Limits of Internal Devaluation. *Industrial Law Journal* 41(3): 254–275.

Bartoli, Clelia, ed. 2019. *Inchiesta a Ballarò. Il diritto visto dal margine.* Palermo: Navarra Editore.

Bascetta, Marco. 2013. 'Il feticcio della legalità'. In *Legalità. Per una critica della ideologia Italiana.* Outlet, pp. 16–21.

Benjamin, Walter. 1985. *Fragmente Autobiographische Schriften.* Berlin: Suhrkamp.

Bhandar, Brenna. 2016. Organised State Abandonment: The Meaning of Grenfell. *Critical Legal Thinking* (blog). http://criticallegalthinking.com/2018/09/21/organised-state-abandonment-the-meaning-of-greenfell.

Bravetti, Federica. 2017. Incontro cittadino a Palermo: verso un Regolamento. *Labsus* (blog). www.labsus.org/2017/12/palermo-verso-un-regolamento-per-la-cura-dei-beni-comuni-2.

Brown, Wendy. 2015. *Undoing the Demos: Neoliberalism's Stealth Revolution.* New York: Zone Books.

Bukowski, Wolf. 2019. *La buona educazione degli oppressi. Piccola storia del decoro.* Rome: Edizioni Alegre.

Cabot, Heath. 2016. "Contagious" Solidarity: Reconfiguring Care and Citizenship in Greece's Social Clinics. *Social Anthropology* 24(2): 152–166.

Chatterjee, Partha. 2004. *The Politics of the Governed: Popular Politics in Most of the World.* New York: Columbia University Press.

Coccoli, Lorenzo. 2017. *Il governo dei poveri all'inizio dell'età moderna. Riforma delle istituzioni assistenziali e dibattiti sulla povertà nell'Europa del Cinquecento.* Sesto San Giovanni: Jouvence.

Colao, Floriana. 2013. *Giustizia e politica. Il processo penale nell'Italia repubblicana.* Milan: Giuffrè.

Colombo, Dario and Enrico Gargiulo. 2016. Participation and Privatisation in Neoliberal Policies: The Case of Italian "Piani Di Zona". *Partecipazione e conflitto* 9(2): 414–440.

Conelli, Carmine. 2022. *Il rovescio della nazione. La costruzione coloniale dell'idea di Mezzogiorno*. Naples: Tamu Edizioni.

Cornelissen, Christoph, Brunello Mantelli and Petra Terhoeven. 2012. *Il decennio rosso. Contestazione sociale e conflitto politico in Germania e in Italia negli anni Sessanta e Settanta*. Bologna: Il Mulino.

Cozzolino, Adriano. 2019. Reconfiguring the State: Executive Powers, Emergency Legislation, and Neoliberalization in Italy. *Globalizations* 16(3): 336–352.

Cuff, Dana. 1998. Community Property: Enter the Architect or, The Politics of Form'. In *Slow Space*, Michael Bell and Sze Tsung Leong (Eds). New York: Monacelli Press.

Dalla Chiesa, Fernando. 1983. Gli studenti contro la mafia: note (di merito) per un movimento. *Quaderni Piacentini* 11: 39–60.

Della Porta, Donatella. 1993. Institutional Responses to Terrorism: The Italian Case. *Terrorism and Political Violence* 4(4): 151–170.

Della Porta, Donatella. 2015. *Social Movements in Times of Austerity: Bringing Capitalism Back Into Protest Analysis*. Cambridge: Polity Press.

Della Porta, Donatella and Sidney Tarrow. 1986. Unwanted Children: Political Violence and the Cycle of Protest in Italy, 1966–1973. *European Journal of Political Research* 14(5–6): 607–632.

Dino, Alessandra. 2005. Sacco di Palermo. *Narcomafie* 11: 183–185.

Dolci, Danilo. 2009. *Banditi a Partinico*. Palermo: Sellerio Editore.

Dolci, Danilo. 2013. *Inchiesta a Palermo*. Palermo: Sellerio Editore.

Elsenbroich, Corinna. 2017. The Addio Pizzo Movement: Exploring Social Change Using Agent-Based Modelling. *Trends in Organized Crime* 20(1): 120–138.

Fava, Ferdinando. 2008. *Lo Zen di Palermo. Antropologia dell'esclusione*. Milan: Franco Angeli.

Foucault, Michel. 1969. *L'archéologie du savoir*. Paris: Gallimard.

Foucault, Michel. 1980. *Power/Knowledge: Selected Interviews and Other Writings 1972–1977*. Brighton: Harvester.

Foucault, Michel. 2008. *The Birth of Biopolitics: Lectures at the Collège de France, 1978–1979*, Michael Senellart (Ed.). New York: Palgrave Macmillan.

Foucault, Michel. 2009. *Security, Territory, Population: Lectures at the Collège de France 1977–1978*, Michael Senellart, François Ewald, and Alessandro Fontana (Eds). London: Palgrave Macmillan.

Frazzica, Giovanni, Valentina Punzo and Attilio Scaglione. 2015. *Non è più quella di una volta. La mafia e le attività estorsive in Sicilia*. Soveria Mannelli: Rubbettino.

Gargiulo, Enrico and Adriano Cirulli. 2016. Gli spazi occupati a Napoli. Informalità, trasformazioni urbane e discorsi sui "beni comuni". In *Società, Economia e Spazio a Napoli. Esplorazioni e Riflessioni*, Working Papers, Gabriella Punziano (Ed.). L'Aquila: GSSI Social Sciences, pp. 85–96.

Giubilaro, Chiara. 2017. Undoing Commons. Diritto alla città, attivismo culturale e pratiche di (Un-)commoning nel sud d'Italia. *ACME: An International Journal for Critical Geographies* 17(2): 325–347.

Giubilaro, Chiara. 2019. Resistenze imperfette. Trasformazioni socio-spaziali a Ballarò (Palermo). In *Territori e resistenze. Spazi in divenire, forme del conflitto e politiche del quotidiano*, Luca Sterchele, Luca Bertoni and Fulvio Biddau (Eds). Trento: Manifestolibri, pp. 41–59.

Gordon, Colin. 1991. Governmental Rationality: An Introduction. In *The Foucault Effect. Studies in Governmentality*, Chicago, IL: University of Chicago Press.

Gramsci, Antonio and Eric J. Hobsbawm. 2000. *The Antonio Gramsci Reader: Selected Writings 1916–1935*, David Forgacs (Ed.). New York: New York University Press.

Guzzini, Stefano. 1995. The "Long Night of the First Republic": Years of Clientelistic Implosion in Italy. *Review of International Political Economy* 2(1): 27–61.

Hall, Stuart. 1992. The West and the Rest: Discourse and Power. In *The Formations of Modernity*, Stuart Hall and Bram Gieben (Eds). Cambridge: Polity Press, pp. 184–227.

Harvey, David. 2008. The Right to the City. *New Left Review* (53): 23–40.

Harvey, David. 2013. *Rebel Cities: From the Right to the City to the Urban Revolution.* 1st edition. London: Verso.

Istituto Nazionale di Statistica. 2023. In crescita la povertà assoluta a causa dell'inflazione (report).

Kaika, Maria. 2017. Between Compassion and Racism: How the Biopolitics of Neoliberal Welfare Turns Citizens into Affective "Idiots". *European Planning Studies* 25(8): 1275–1291.

Kelty, Christopher M. 2016. Too Much Democracy in All the Wrong Places: Toward a Grammar of Participation. *Current Anthropology* 58(15): 77–90.

Liang, Lawrence. 2005. 'Porous Legalities and Avenues of Participation'. *Sarai Reader 2005: Bare Acts*: 6–17.

Lucarelli, Alberto. 2013. *La democrazia dei beni comuni. Nuove frontiere del diritto pubblico*. Bari: Laterza.

Lupo, Salvatore. 2004. *Storia della mafia: dalle origini ai giorni nostri*. Rome: Donzelli Editore.

Marx, Karl. 1970. *Critique of Hegel's Philosophy of Right*. First ed. 1843. Cambridge, MA: Cambridge University Press.

Massey, Doreen. 2013. Vocabularies of the Economy. *Soundings* 54: 9–22.

Mazzenzana, Sarah, ed. 2016. Il maxiprocesso di Palermo. *Rivista di studi e ricerche sulla criminalità organizzata* 2(1): 117–169.

Mezzadra, Sandro. 2007. *La condizione postcoloniale. Storia e politica nel mondo globale*. Verona: Ombre Corte.

Micciarelli, Giuseppe. 2021. 'Path for New Institutions and Urban Commons. Legal and Political Acts for the Recognition of Urban Civic and Collective Use Starting from Naples'. Urbact.

Montagna, Nicola. 2006. The De-Commodification of Urban Space and the Occuped Social Centers in Italy. *City* 10(3): 295–304.

Montagnani, Francesco. 2020. "Un po' di gentrificazione però ci voleva..." Dubbi e certezze sul rinnovamento urbano. *Etnografie del contemporaneo* 3(3): 63–74.

Muehlebach, Andrea. 2012. *The Moral Neoliberal: Welfare and Citizenship in Italy*. Chicago, IL: The University of Chicago Press.

Muehlebach, Andrea. 2013. The Catholicization of Neoliberalism: On Love and Welfare in Lombardy, Italy. *American Anthropologist* 115(3): 452–465.

Nivarra, Luca. 2008. *Gli anni Settanta del diritto privato. Atti del convegno. Palermo, 7–8 Luglio 2006*. Milan: Giuffrè.

Nobili, Massimo. 1998. *Scenari e trasformazioni del processo penale*. Milan: Cedam.

Orlando, Leoluca. 2000. From a Culture of Lawfulness to an Economy of Legality. International Symposium on 'The Role of Civil Society: Creating a Culture of Lawfulness; The Palermo, Sicily Renaissance'. Palermo.

Partridge, Henry. 2012. The Determinants of and Barriers to Critical Consumption: A Study of Addiopizzo. *Modern Italy* 17(3): 343–363.

Pecile, Veronica. 2017. Urban Mobilisations in a Post-Crisis Mediterranean City: The Case of Commons in Palrmo. *Comparative Law Review* 8(1): 31–46.

Pecile, Veronica. 2022. Between Urban Commons and Touristification: Radical and Conservative Uses of the Law in Post-Austerity Southern Italy. *City – Analysis of Urban Change, Theory, Action* 26 (5–6): 998–1011.

Polanyi, Karl. 1957. *The Great Transformation: The Political and Economic Origins of Our Time*. Princeton, NJ: Beacon Press.

Quarta, Alessandra. 2016. *Non proprietà: teoria e prassi dell'accesso ai beni*. Naples: Edizioni Scientifiche Italiane.

Renda, Francesco. 1993. *Resistenza alla mafia come movimento nazionale*. Soveria Mannelli: Rubbettino Editore.

Rescigno, Giuseppe Ugo. 2016. Principio di legalità. *Diritto on line*. www.treccani.it/enciclopedia/principio-di-legalita_%28Diritto-on-line%29.

Roura-Expósito, Joan and Pablo Alonso González. 2018. Too Little Democracy in All the Right Places. *Current Anthropology* 59(3): 332–333.

Santino, Umberto. 2000. *Storia del movimento antimafia. Dalla lotta di classe all'impegno civile*. Rome: Editori Riuniti.

Sassoon, Donald. 1995. Tangentopoli or the Democratization of Corruption: Considerations on the End of Italy's First Republic. *Journal of Modern Italian Studies* 1 (1): 124–143.

Schneider, Jane and Peter T. Schneider. 1976. *Culture and Political Economy in Western Sicily*. New York, San Francisco and London: Academic Press.

Schneider, Jane and Peter T. Schneider. 1996. Dalle guerre contadine alle guerre urbane: il movimento antimafia a Palermo. *Meridiana* (25): 47–75.

Schneider, Jane and Peter T. Schneider. 2001. Civil Society Versus Organized Crime: Local and Global Perspectives. *Critique of Anthropology* 21(4): 427–446.

Schneider, Jane and Peter T. Schneider. 2003. *Reversible Destiny: Mafia, Antimafia, and the Struggle for Palermo*. Berkeley, CA: University of California Press.

Sciascia, Leonardo. 1987. I professionisti dell'antimafia. *Il Corriere della Sera*. http://old.radicali.it/search_view.php?id=49224.

Spanò, Michele. 2017. La normatività dei governati. Un tracciato post-coloniale. *Scienza & Politica* 29(57): 247–269.

Spanò, Michele and Alessandra Quarta. 2017. Istituire la cooperazione. Dentro e contro la crisi. In *Rispondere alla crisi. Comune, cooperazione sociale e diritto*, Michele Spanò and Alessandra Quarta (Eds). Verona: Ombre Corte.

Standing, Guy. 2011. *The Precariat: The New Dangerous Class*. London: Bloomsbury Academic.

Svimez. 2011. *Rapport Svimez 2011 Sull'economia Del Mezzogiorno*. Bologna: Il Mulino.

Tilly, Charles. 1978. *From Mobilization to Revolution*. Reading, MA: Addison-Wesley.

Tilly, Charles. 1998. *Durable Inequality*. Berkeley, CA: University of California Press.

Todeschini, Giacomo. 2007. *Visibilmente crudeli. Malviventi, persone sospette e gente qualunque dal medioevo all'età moderna*. Bologna: Il Mulino.

Tonanzi, Roberta. 2020. Regolamento sulla collaborazione tra cittadini e amministrazioni per la cura, la rigenerazione e la gestione condivisa dei beni comuni urbani. *Labsus, laboratorio per la sussidiarietà*. www.labsus.org/2024/06/dieci-anni-dopo-un-nuovo-prototipo-del-regolamento/.

Tronconi, Filippo. 2015. *Beppe Grillo's Five Star Movement: Organisation, Communication and Ideology*. First ed. London: Routledge.

Varese, Federico. 2013. Protezione ed estorsione. *Kainos — Rivista on line di critica filosofica*. www.kainos-portale.com/index.php/12-malavita/86-ricerche12/304-protezione-ed-estorsione.

Weber, Max. 2010. *The Protestant Ethic and the Spirit of Capitalism*. Translated by Stephen Kalberg. Oxford: Oxford University Press.

Wulff Barreiro, Federico and Oscar Brito Gonzalez. 2020. The Production of Intercultural Urban Landscapes, a Multi-Scalar Approach: The Case of Ballarò, Palermo. *Urban Design International* 25(3): 250–265.

Legal sources

Comune di Palermo. 2017a. 'Atto d'indirizzo politico – Avvio processo di formalizzazione regolata e definita del fenomeno: "Mercato dell'usato e del libero scambio nel quartiere Albergheria" (Deliberazione della Giunta Comunale n. 81 del 21/04/2017).

Comune di Palermo. 2017b. 'Atto d'indirizzo politico – Modello dell'"uso civico collettivo urbano" presso il complesso del teatro Montevergini' (Deliberazione della Giunta Comunale n. 74 del 13/04/2017).

Comune di Palermo. 2019. 'Atto d'indirizzo politico – Avvio del "mercato dell'usato e del libero scambio nel quartiere Albergheria" – linee guida (Deliberazione della Giunta Municipale n. 120 del 03/07/2019).

Comune di Palermo. 2023. 'Regolamento sulla collaborazione tra cittadini e amministrazione per la cura, la rigenerazione e la gestione condivisa dei beni comuni' (Deliberazione di Consiglio Comunale n. 31 del 20/04/2023).

Chapter 2

On the politics of the commons

beni comuni as an empty signifier and Southern Italian neoliberalism

De-romanticising the commons

In this chapter, I draw on the mobilisations resumed in Chapter 1 to suggest some insights about the politics of the commons that could to be the object of future critical inquiry. In the first section, I concentrate on the features of a politics of the commons emerging from the analysed practices, focusing on the traits of the groups reclaiming them. I argue that in the post-2008 crisis phase, the commons functioned as an empty signifier evoked by different subjects advancing a variety of social demands and trying to realise diverse political projects in the same spaces at a time of profound social and economic change. Collective access to spaces and wealth redistribution are only some of the goals pursued by actors reclaiming the commons and existed alongside other kinds of claims and visions of society that were advanced in the name of them. Southern Italian cities provide an instance of the clash that can take place among different subjects regarding the modes of conceiving the commons as ideas for accessing and governing urban space. At stake in this negotiation is the very political content of the commons and, as I will clarify in the following chapters, their legal meaning, which hardly coalesces into one consistent regime. I maintain that groups mobilising for the commons differ significantly from the concept of an autonomous community posited by much of critical scholarship as the main agent of the commons, In light of the Palermo example, I challenge the idea of the commons as a sphere that would exist separately from the public and the private realm and argue for their deep entanglement with both, an entwinement reflected by the exchange of discourses and practices developed under the label of "commons" that involved actors entertain with state and market structures. Doing a critique of the commons thus brings to recognise autonomy as the constant involvement of the subjects reclaiming them in the negotiation of social and legal structures.

Drawing on these two elements – the commons as an empty signifier and the groups taking care of them as far from coinciding with the autonomous community – the chapter then contextualises the politics of the Southern

DOI: 10.4324/9781003335320-3

Italian commons in the broader scenario of the late capitalist transformations reshaping Southern Europe after the 2008 economic breakdown. The focus shifts to a critical reading of the public policies through which urban space was reorganised in Southern Italian cities during the 2010s. As will be explained, these measures borrowed discursive and practical elements from the mobilisations for the commons and were embedded in a national policy framework centred on a governmental notion of *beni comuni* as key for reorganising and disciplining urban space. Policies such as those promoting the restoration of historic buildings, the regeneration of market areas and the expansion of public housing were important axes for restructuring cities to make them more apt for tourism. A crucial element for the implementation of these policies was the local state's capacity to incorporate discourses and practices of the commons into its bureaucratic structures.

The third and final section introduces a further level of analysis regarding the nature of the capitalist transformation occurring in this region in the 2010s. I maintain that in cities of the Italian South, new processes of value extraction target precisely what part of the mobilisation for the commons sought to protect, namely the everyday life of the popular classes living in the historic areas and appearing as authentic, unique, folkloric to the outside gaze of tourists and investors. The alleged backwardness of Southern Italian societies vis-à-vis the developed and progressive North – a discourse that has been characterising Italian modernisation since its very outset – has thus become the object of accumulation. While Southern otherness has long been the spirit of Italian capitalism, what is new is that the commodification of such alterity becomes the fundamental logic for reorganising urban space. The methodological cue offered is that local trajectories of the commons provide a lens to read the logics of late capitalist reconfiguration. In this metamorphosis, the commons and those who reclaim them are both the object of co-optation attempts and a powerful engine of discourses and practices of resistance.

The commons as an empty signifier: one term, different social demands

Dismissing the myth of the autonomous community

Critical scholarship focusing on urban social movements in the post-2008 phase has built a fairly coherent imaginary when it comes to providing a political interpretation of the mobilisations for the commons. In the field of urban geography, the commons are conceived as "the very spaces, materials and practices that possess or have acquired a certain autonomy from capital and/or the state", as the bulwark of an "autonomous city" that can break the link between urbanisation and capitalist accumulation (Vasudevan 2015: 318–329). Social movement studies focusing on Southern European movements opposing austerity policies posit the commons as a realm existing beyond the public and the private spheres – a "self-organising praxis" radically challenging the existing socio-economic order (Sabariego 2022: 189). Even in feminist approaches framing the commons as spaces of social reproduction and ecological imagination we find the thesis that the logic underpinning the commons would be to imagine a postcapitalist order beyond the state and the market (Caffentzis and Federici 2014; Sato and Soto Alarcón 2019). In the field of critical legal studies, scholars point to the commons as an instance of how property can be reconceived in relational terms, as a bond between individuals and things not based on possessive individualism, if the emphasis in the legal construction is put on the side of the community's interests (Cooper 2007; Mattei 2011; Davies 2012).

A point that these studies share is the centrality of a community conceived in specific terms. What this scholarship posits is the existence of an autonomous group at the core of the commons, one acting away from state and market logics. According to these approaches, individuals would turn to the commons to counter the effects of "too much capitalism" on their lives. Some post-Marxist scholars go as far as to see in these actors the reemergence of Marx's revolutionary subjectivity (Harrison 2014). For instance, the notion of the multitude points to the rise of a collective actor that announces the passage to a post-capitalist stage and to the commons as the pivotal space to achieve this transition (Hardt and Negri 2009; De Angelis 2010).

Some voices within the debate question this idea of the community as a pure, transhistorical subject acting in a generic "outside" realm and prefiguring the fall of the capitalist order. Feminist scholars, in particular, prefer to focus on commoning as the circular relationship between a thing and a group taking care of it, which allows framing the commons as spaces of social reproduction (Linebaugh 2008; Federici 2010; Clement et al. 2019). Furthermore, a broad philosophical debate has been rejecting conceptions of the community that reduce it to an essence.[1] However, this critical work fails to grasp an aspect that emerges in the politics of the commons of the diverse practices reviewed in Chapter 1. Far from acting in isolation, groups that reclaim the commons to pursue any political project concerning the urban space entertained a tactic and instrumental relation with both state and market actors. One way of reading the Palermo story of the commons is a dismissal of the romantic visions of the community that much of the

1 Essentialist visions of the community have been thoroughly undermined in continental philosophical debates. See, among others, Jean-Luc Nancy's work on the nostalgia for archaic communities as a trait of Western modern thought and inspiring many political projects, including Marxist ones (Nancy 1983); Giorgio Agamben's concept of the *qualunque* – a human being who has no historical or spiritual destiny to fulfil – as the basis for future communities (Agamben 1990); and Roberto Esposito's reconceptualisation of the community as based on reciprocal gifts (Esposito 1998).

scholarship on the subject has advanced. The reclaiming of the commons is deeply embedded in the contingencies of the socio-economic transformations affecting each context. Such changes unfold through complex and case-specific networks of conflicts, alliances, transformative and disciplinary attitudes towards urban space – an interplay in which the commons take on a shifting role. In the practices that took place in Palermo under the label of the commons, it was difficult to identify a subject that resembled an autonomous community acting as a homogeneous and ordered group entirely beyond the state and market logics. What emerged was a different kind of setting in which, to use Foucault's terms, power and resistance were so closely intertwined that resistance could precede power and alter its course, in a circular way.[2] Only with this idea in mind is it possible to start deciphering, at least in part, the tortuous interactions between activists mobilising for the commons and public authorities. The complexity of this dialectic is difficult to disentangle, but it certainly contradicts the idea of a separation of the commons from public and private logics. Instead, what is observable is the circulation of discourses and practices of the commons between the public, the private and the activist spheres – admitting that any neat boundary can be drawn to separate them – to enact different political projects concerning the same urban space.

Palermo's groups reclaiming the commons

In the Palermo case, both the occupations of cultural spaces and the urban renewal efforts led by citizen groups are at odds with ideas of autonomous community. As for the first ones, the most emblematic practice being the occupation of the Garibaldi Theatre, activists openly reclaimed a link with the national and international struggle for the commons. Unlike other national cases, such as the Valle Theatre, in which occupants organised as a legal subject by establishing a private law foundation, these occupations reached an end before activists could resort to law to institute their use of the spaces and thus provide continuity to their self-government practices. The occupants had a twofold political reference inspiring their actions, namely, the history of the country's *centri sociali* and a cycle of anti-austerity mobilisations that in Italy had started with the Wave (Ruggiero 2000; Mudu 2015). In these cases, reclaiming the commons meant demanding a right to occupy and use cultural spaces according to their established function – a use made ever more necessary by the conditions of economic recession and welfare cuts. These activities were carried out through an engagement not only with the local administration but also with the private sphere, as proved by the self-branding practices adopted in

2 "If there was no resistance, there would be no power relations. [...] So resistance comes first, and resistance remains superior to the other forces of the process; power relations are obliged to change with the resistance" (Foucault 1996: 386).

the case of the cultural warehouses to attract external support. Rethinking culture as a commons did not mean situating it beyond a private/public horizon but withdrawing it from privatisation and reclaiming the collective access to spaces in which culture is produced outside the logic of competition and profit.

Regarding the urban renovation practices led by groups inspired by anti-mafia values, another idea of the commons was at play. These efforts were part of the complex history of the anti-mafia movement in the second half of the twentieth century and of its increasing focus on the cultural and educational side of the fight against organised crime. Taking over the urban space was of particular importance, also from a symbolic point of view, to rebalance power in favour of citizens. What is "common" here was the space subtracted from the mafia and administered according to *legalità* and *civismo*. Citizen committees and associations devoted to such values were good allies for public administrations willing to carve into stone their dissociation from mafia power. In this case, the commons are the core of a collective identity, that of a civil society composed of middle- and upper-class individuals – professionals, entrepreneurs, public servants – that uses the urban space in an ethical way. The risk, though, in the absence of a class-conscious analysis on the side of the civil society, is of perpetuating the urban inequalities all the while defending social order, which, as De Angelis reminds us, is always done by supporting policies "for 'better' government, for 'nicer' environment, for 'less' poverty, for 'improved' public services" (De Angelis 2010: 964).

The community at the heart of the SOS Ballarò experience also differs from the ideal of the autonomous community and for reasons other than those just outlined. In this case, the commons are the name for a reclaiming of spaces made in the interest of a population existing beyond the realm of civil society. SOS Ballarò is a collective subject kept together by a method, that of assembly, used to defend the property interests of the political society in an area epitomising the effects of the socio-economic transformation undergone by the cities of the Italian South at that juncture. The resort to assemblies as a method to democratise social movements and deconstruct centralised ideas of leadership was a shared trait among anti-austerity protests in the aftermath of the 2008 crisis (Hardt and Negri 2017). As outlined in Chapter 1, SOS Ballarò adopted assembly both to oppose the stigma attributed to the neighbourhood and to counter the marginalisation affecting the residents that was accelerated by the adoption of a tourism-based economic model. Its reference was not only the wave of assembly-based mobilisations against austerity worldwide but also the forms of urban resistance developing in several Southern European cities during the 2010s, which, besides opposing budget cuts, built collective responses to the exclusionary and xenophobic management of state welfare by institutions (Kaika 2017). SOS Ballarò can be contextualised in this framework of practices aimed at protecting the right to a dignified existence of the precarious, who were made even more precarious in the context of austerity. What was preserved by the public assembly were the "normative conditions that must be fulfilled for life to become life" (Butler 2004: 39). At the same time, SOS Ballarò went beyond the scope of the anti-austerity struggles and pursued contingent goals that implied significant uses of the law. To challenge the structural conditions of poverty and exclusion affecting the residents, the assembly acted not only at the level of discourse – dismissing the common sense stigmatising the neighbourhood and promoting a new image of it, in which the historical identity of the vendors is at the core of Ballarò's social fabric – but also on another level, that of the legal regime regulating the uses of public spaces. By directly intervening in the formulation of the legal tools disciplining Ballarò's spaces, activists manipulated the concepts through which, using Bourdieu's terms, space is constructed and governed (Bourdieu 1989).

Even the practices conducted in the name of the commons in the self-governed medical clinic initiated by the collective of Anomalia went in the same direction of protecting the city's political society from the erosion of its livelihood. What was reclaimed as a commons in this case was health, and to this aim, the right of the most marginalised to receive medical treatments and live a dignified life. Moreover, by highlighting how illness has a political dimension, and all the more so at a time when public welfare is being eroded, the proposed project had to do not only with the self-government of spaces, but also with the possibility of imagining forms of non-state welfare based on a principle of solidarity.

Finally, in the case of the Montevergini Theatre, it is again culture that was reclaimed as a commons during its privatisation. However, unlike the case of the Garibaldi Theatre, the experience of Montevergini was characterised by a tactic use of law by activists following the virtuous example of the ex-Asilo Filangieri in Naples. Reviving an old institution such as that of civic uses proved timely to protect the collective use and access to spaces where rights are realised.

Another aspect that should be highlighted is how the partial channelling of radical demands into the more moderate political agenda of the state actor, which is observable in the analysed practices, is a typical moment of any mobilisation's life course. This does not imply the complete absorption of the claims for the commons by the state. Social movement studies have long stressed that the co-optation of a movement's leadership by local elites is quite a frequent outcome (Piven and Cloward 1977). Gaining elite support, even at the cost of watering down demands, is crucial for activists to ensure the movement's survival, especially in moments of low activity or internal conflict. Besides, there are circumstances in which the movement's institutionalisation is inevitable not only to endure but even to influence mainstream politics (Cress and Snow 1996). Thus, in order to survive in the public sphere, activists may choose to scale down their demands and adapt them to the existing institutional framework. This does not necessarily happen through the absorption of movement members into institutions, but also, in a more nuanced way, through the institutional endorsement of movements' goals and tactics (NeJaime 2013).

This reflection brings us to another point, namely, the capacity of the public actor to exert a dominant role in the classification of practices taking place in the public space (Bourdieu 1989). However, the trajectory of the commons explored in Chapter 1 shows that how this process unfolds in a late capitalist city is far from linear. Certainly, it recalls David Harvey's definition of urbanisation as "a spatially grounded social process in which a wide range of different actors with quite different objectives and agendas interact through a particular configuration of interlocking spatial practices", capable of creating "institutional arrangements, legal forms, political and administrative systems, hierarchies of power, and the like" (Harvey 1989: 5). Nevertheless, this nonlinear trajectory shows how the formulation of institutional arrangements, forms and systems is the result of a negotiation between actors that by the same category – the commons – imply entirely different practices and visions of the city.

In sum, occupied cultural spaces, anti-mafia regeneration practices, an assembly defending the interests of the political society, a self-governed medical structure: these experiences differed in many respects, from the political culture inspiring them to the methods adopted by their activists. What they shared is the divergence of the groups from the ideal type of the autonomous community and a shared appeal to the commons as a label to legitimise diverse social claims. The commons functioned as an empty signifier, as defined by Ernesto Laclau: an umbrella demand able to catalyse diverse social claims into one seemingly consistent assertion. Because it succeeds in representing the totality of such demands, the empty signifier, in itself particular, ends up taking on a universal meaning. It becomes a common denominator of social life through which hegemony is built (Laclau 2005; Gargiulo and Cirulli 2016). In the case of Palermo, this struggle for hegemony concerned how spaces should be used and accessed in the post-2008 crisis restructuring. As will be discussed in the next chapter, law plays a crucial role in establishing which modes of use and access to urban space become predominant and does so by framing the commons in different ways.

Neoliberalism seen from the Italian South: public policies in the name of the commons

Neoliberalism from below in the Italian South

It is now worth looking at the realm of public policy and at how the projects for urban renewal led by local elites interacted with ideas and practices of the commons. Before doing this, it is important to clarify what this book means by a neoliberal scenario and the power dynamic that underpins it. Wendy Brown frames neoliberalism as a peculiar, yet "inconsistent and differentiated" reason that remakes each aspect of life in economic terms thereby hampering the grounds of democracy, whose elements concur to turn the political character of democracy's founding elements into economic ones (Brown 2015: 17–20). Neoliberalism can be seen as a rationality, as Foucault argues, intended as the mode of organising and regulating conducts peculiar to late capitalism, and it implies a radical reorganisation of the relations between the state and society (Dardot and Laval 2014). In *Neoliberalism as Exception*, Aihwa Ong suggests that an ethnographic approach is helpful to disentangle the specific ways in which market, sovereignty and citizenship get reconfigured and intertwined in late capitalist scenarios (Ong 2006). Her work has the quality of empirically illustrating the diverse, even counterintuitive modes, in which this reorganisation takes place (Spanò 2013).

The story of the commons in Palermo is emblematic of how the neoliberal rationality proceeded in the years following the 2008 economic crisis in the cities of the Italian South. Two theoretical insights, both coming from the field of critical geography, support this reading: the thesis of studying social movements in European "borderlands" as critical for an epistemological renewal of social sciences beyond a perspective based on the global North (Baptista 2013); and the idea that the impact of austerity policies can be assessed through an ethnographic focus on urban movements (Tulumello 2016).

Grassroots practices and public policies carried out under the label of the commons in Palermo in the 2010s thus provide a precious vantage point from which to observe how the neoliberal reshaping of urban economies and societies of the Italian South occurred at that conjuncture. This restructuring did not proceed in a linear and top-down way. There was no such thing as a monolithic "power" – no external direction that determined in any absolute way the behaviour of the involved actors. On the contrary, investigating these transformations from below, from the level of social mobilisations and struggles, revealed the emergence of new subjectivities and disclosed a multiplicity of forms of resistance and lines of flight. Neoliberal governmentality is continually distorted and revived by those who both endure and appropriate it (Mezzadra 2023: 9). Veronica Gago's concept of neoliberalism from below is useful to describe the non-linearity of this process. In her study of the informal market of La Salada in Buenos Aires, a border land separating the city from its province built on the initiative of migrants and grown after the 2001 economic crisis that hit Argentina, Gago argues that understanding contemporary neoliberalism requires "focusing on its capacity for mutation, its dynamic of permanent variation, especially looking at variations in meaning, at recursive, nonlinear time rhythms, at disruption driven by social struggles" (Gago 2017: 5). Neoliberal transformations certainly occur "from above", as strategies deployed by governments and private actors through which global regimes of accumulation change. But they also take place "from below", through the spread of forms of life in which the meanings of freedom, citizenship and obedience are altered and recombined. Gago highlights that the interplay between neoliberalism and informal economies is not a straightforward one: the former does not exclude the latter, quite the contrary. The economic activities conducted in the market space on which capitalist valorisation draws are highly heterogeneous. The market is thus both a place of resistance and exploitation, traversed by contradictory drives through which subaltern subjects come to terms with neoliberal rationality without being its mere victims. In the case of Palermo, the targets of valorisation are not the economic activities conducted in the market per se but the very existence and form of life of the popular classes.

After revising the use of the concept of the commons by citizen groups and mobilisations, it is now time to look at the public discourses, policies and norms adopted at the state level having at their core a sanitised, civic vision of the commons, which partly co-opts the notion of *beni comuni* developed at the grassroots level. It is helpful to recall a public statement made by the mayor of Palermo in 2015, when the city council signed a document establishing the concession of the area of Piazzetta Mediterraneo on free loan to the municipality by the Catholic Church. In this declaration, the mayor commented on the municipality's decision to support the bottom-up process of urban regeneration of activists in Piazzetta Mediterraneo, in Ballarò, by connecting these practices to values of legality and citizenship:

> The acquisition of this space in the heart of Ballarò is part of a series of initiatives led by the city council to promote all activities aimed at social development, growth of social spaces and strong need for legality in some areas of Palermo. It also aims to strengthen the citizens' sense of belonging to the neighbourhoods that represent the soul of this city. The management of this space allows the continuation of the regeneration efforts spontaneously initiated by a group of residents and places them in the framework of a public-private synergy aimed at the recovery of the historic centre.[3]

Renovation of historic buildings

One of the most important urban renewal policies pursued by the municipality of Palermo in the 2010s was the restoration of the historical heritage, an objective sealed by the approval of a three-year plan in 2019. This document had a twofold objective: the refurbishment of public buildings bearing a historical and artistic value and the implementation of measures to improve the touristic offer. The plan, drawn up by the city's Department of Urban Regeneration, identified specific restoration work to be carried out in the coming years in public palaces and churches.[4] After the 2008 crisis, the strengthening of

3 'Albergheria, piazzetta Mediterraneo rinascerà come area verde': www.palermotoday.it/cronaca/albergheria-piazzetta-mediterraneo-comune-area-verde.html.

the tourism economy and of a robust urban regeneration market capable of attracting private capital in Southern European cities has not implied a laissez-faire attitude of the public actor, but rather an interventionist state machine (Brenner et al. 2013; Mendes 2018). The tourism-based economic renaissance of Southern Italian cities in this period was based on public urban regeneration projects that relied heavily on a disciplinary concept of the commons. Palermo's urban redevelopment plan was adopted within a broader policy framework that promoted the tourism-led transformation of urban economies in the Italian *Mezzogiorno*. An Operational Plan for Culture and Tourism (*piano operativo Cultura e Turismo*) was approved by the national government to cover the post-crisis years between 2014 and 2020. One of its stated objectives was to increase the "touristic fruition" of the "urban systems" of Southern Italian cities: 90 million euros were earmarked for the restoration of the four historic centres of Palermo, Naples, Taranto and Cosenza. The plan urged the creation of a system of "multilevel governance" and the involvement of "territorial communities" in the decision-making process prior to intervention, using methods based on "public debate". Emphasis was placed on the aims of "real estate renewal, mobility, quality of the commons and urban decorum". The basis for designing the plan was the legislation on ad hoc policies and a wider government project for the Italian South, the *Grande Progetto Destinazione Sud*, which aimed to achieve economic development through the promotion of the cultural and artistic heritage and the expansion of tourism, by "actively involving the territory's stakeholders in a participatory perspective", as stated in ministerial documents (Ministero della Cultura 2018).

These policies, adopted at the end of a decade marked by the severe economic and social impact of the crisis, which disproportionately affected the South, envisaged a national renaissance based on tourism anchored in a particular conception of the commons, one linked with real estate renewal, participatory processes and urban decorum. In order to achieve the objectives of this policy, the government explicitly encouraged synergies between public and private actors at the national and local level.[5]

4 From the website of the municipality: www.comune.palermo.it/js/server/uploads/_02072019061042.pdf.

5 An example of public-private urban regeneration project in Palermo took place in the popular neighbourhood of Danisinni. The municipality agreed with Airbnb to deduct a fee from each booking and use the money to fund two projects selected through an online survey. The two winning projects, an artists' residency and a social kitchen, were based on themes – art and food – that act as classic triggers for value extraction. While the spread of art spaces is a feature of early gentrification in peripheral neighbourhoods, to the point that scholars speak of "art-driven space domestication" as a mode of organising urban space (Sacco et al. 2019), food has become a key element in the post-crisis reconstruction of the touristic attractiveness of Italian cities (Sassatelli et al. 2015).

Regeneration of the historic markets

A second policy axis aimed at renewing the city's image and economy in the 2010s was the regeneration of the historic markets, of which Ballarò is one. In Palermo, the *Regolamento Unico dei Mercati Generali* (Unified Regulation for General Markets) was approved by the city council in 2019 and regulates the food and fish markets replacing two older instruments adopted in 1964 and 1971. This tool strengthened the public control in market areas to prevent illegal sales and enforced higher hygiene standards, in an attempt to make markets fit for their new function as tourist attractions in the urban economy (Comune di Palermo 2019). Other examples of legal instruments adopted by the municipality for the renovation of market areas and their economic role are the two regulations on the Ballarò market, approved in 2017 and 2019 as a result of negotiations with the public assembly. As mentioned in the previous chapter, the first tool recognises the role of the re-use market as a social safety net for people in conditions of socio-economic marginalisation and grants the vendors the status of vendors by need, while the second instrument recognises the guidelines for the shared government of the market area proposed by the assembly. What has been achieved, then, is greater protection for the vendors' interests in the market space and the recognition of the social and cultural value of the market alongside its economic value, in an attempt to reconnect the wealth create in the market with the people who generate it.

It is still too early to understand the long-term effects of this regularisation. It would be tempting to link this operation to the discourses of powerful private subjects calling for urban decency and the exclusion of street vendors from the historic centre through ad hoc municipal orders. In 2019, the local Chamber of Commerce urged the municipality to take action against street vendors, claiming that their activities were detrimental to the renewed image of Palermo. In a letter to the mayor, the chamber's representative complained that the vendors had "flooded" the districts on the outskirts of the city after they were banned from selling in the historic areas, an order issued after the centre was declared a UNESCO World Heritage Site.[6] This legalistic discourse, punitive towards the reality of the material conditions in which a large part of the inhabitants of the historic centre live, overlooked the fact that the co-existence of regular and informal economic options is a condition for the cohabitation of different social classes (Saitta 2019).

Another possible issue is that the system of fixed posts could hamper the market's role as social safety net, as it was unclear what mechanisms would be used to make room for newcomers who wanted to settle and start their activities in the market. This decision recalls, albeit on another scale and in a

6 'Confcommercio contro i venditori ambulanti: "Troppe bancarelle danneggiano la città"': www.palermotoday.it/cronaca/bancarelle-venditori-ambulanti-lettera-confcommercio-comune.html.

different context, of the policies implemented by international agencies such as the World Bank in the Global South, inspired by Hernando de Soto's ideas on property rights. In these scenarios, titling policies were applied with the conviction that the inclusion of squatters in the legal economic circuits would automatically improve their living conditions (De Soto 2000; Esquirol 2017).

Despite such potential criticisms, it is also possible that in the long term the regularisation of market areas could redistribute wealth, reduce poverty and protect access to public space. Importantly, it could give activists the confidence to experiment more with the law – a theme explored in the next chapter. In Southern Italian cities, the reformalisation of market areas could provide the core for a larger plan of grassroots urban regeneration, with activists acting as a mediating force between the marginalised residents and public authorities in a way that protects the interests of the former (Pecile 2022).

Public housing

A third policy area for renewing urban space in which ideas of the commons were at stake was a domain crucial for implementing a neoliberal agenda at the urban level, i.e., housing (Tulumello 2016). Scholarship has highlighted how in contemporary cities, the housing sector exerts an important macroeconomic function that has more to do with stabilising the rental market than realising a right to housing for all. For the sake of urban renewal, evictions are carried out by public authorities with the result of undermining the very possibility of survival for the marginalised (Rolnik 2019; Rossi 2022). In the 2010s, Palermo was affected by a housing emergency that threatened the livelihood of the popular classes, just as many other cities in the Italian South and austerity-hit Southern Europe more broadly (Tulumello 2019; Galeota Lanza and De Martino 2022). In 2018, the Italian General Confederation of Labour denounced a dramatic situation in the city, with about six thousand people in a state of homelessness, around 1,300 evictions per year and the waiting list for the assignment of social housing blocked since 2006.[7] In a decision contested by several political forces, the city council conceded to regularise the status of more than 800 families living in squatted buildings. The mayor commented on the move in a public statement underpinned by ideas of the commons:

> In a context like Palermo and Sicily, the problem of squatting does not belong to the sphere of public order and property protection, but to the broader issue of the right to housing. While in the North [of Italy] this

7 This topic was treated at the conference "Abitare, famiglie, sviluppo" held by Sunia (*Sindacato Unitario Nazionale Inquilini Assegnatari*) and CGIL in the church of San Mattia dei Crociferi in Palermo in September 2018.

> phenomenon mainly affects private buildings, in Palermo and Sicily it almost exclusively affects public buildings, mostly public social housing, occupied by residents of our region. […] It remains important to give a signal from the state that this property is available for the community, for [solving] the housing emergency and for social purposes.[8]

Linking the housing emergency to the realisation of the right to housing and not to issues of public order was a sign of political sensitivity towards the residents' material conditions on the part of the municipality. This was also the result of the interaction between the city council and the movements: even in this domain, the municipality welcomed the demands of activists, who had long been calling for an increase in social housing. Working together with the Istituto Autonomo Case Popolari, a public institution advocating for access to social housing, they mediated with the region to provide the long-time occupants a property title to live in occupied housing units, where in most cases they would entitled to stay if the allocation mechanism had not been blocked for years. While real estate renovation and the regularisation of market areas are also conducive to increasing rent values, a careful approach to social housing protects the popular classes by providing them with the infrastructure to remain in the city.

The touristic transformation of the Italian South: extracting value from political society

Having mapped how both grassroots practices and public policies of urban regeneration resort to the concept of the commons to legitimise their attempts at reorganising urban space, it can be helpful to contextualise this contention within the specific capitalist transformation taking place in Southern Italian societies. The 2008 economic breakdown was the occasion for a profound renewal of the capitalist system in this region, a restructuring that thrives on the conditions of precariousness experienced by large parts of the population and is based on extracting value from political society's everyday life.

This transformation takes place through converting urban economies into a tourism-based model. In his critical studies on urban planning and housing policies, Samuel Stein defines tourism as a concept entailing a practical and an ideological dimension. A term useful to describe many of the ways in which value is extracted from cultural forms, affective networks and social cooperation in late capitalist contexts – in other words, an instance of the biopolitical exploitation of labour (Hardt and Negri 2009) – tourism is two things at once: a strategy for reorganising public space and urban economies to satisfy the demands of tourists and investors over those of other users of the public space, such as the poor, the

8 Orlando e Mattina: 'Occupazioni, problema legato a diritto alla casa. A Palermo 850 famiglie avviano regolarizzazione': www.giornalelora.it/orlando-e-mattina-occupazioni-problema-legato-a-diritto-alla-casa-a-palermo-850-famiglie-avviano-regolarizzazion.

migrant and the precarious; but also, and this is where ideology comes in, a set of discourses that present this reconfiguration as legitimate and even desirable for all of the city's residents (Stein 2020).

Tourism conceptualised in this way is useful for making sense of the profound transformation of urban space that activists reclaiming the commons in Palermo found themselves confronted with, and they were not the only ones to face such challenges during the decade of the 2010s. In the years after 2008, several cities in Southern Europe were reshaped to fit an economic model based on tourism, embraced by local elites as a panacea for the effects of recession. The development of tourism in peripheral economies with favourable preconditions – warm climate, presence of coastlines and historical heritage – was also strongly encouraged at the EU level as a strategy to spur economic growth and European integration (Bürgisser and Di Carlo 2023). Some critical international trends, such as the geopolitical turmoil affecting tourist destinations in North Africa and the Middle East in the same years and the emergence of real estate as a paramount investment sector, have contributed to fostering this trend (Sequera and Nofre 2018). This shift towards a tourism monoculture has disrupted the social fabric, causing enclosure of public spaces, erosion of the right to housing, gentrification of neighbourhoods, and environmental harm (Calzada 2020). The resulting scenario, which some called austerity urbanism, has implied a change in the structure of these cities in terms of increasing inequality, and what has been put at risk is the very survival of the most marginalised inhabitants (Peck 2012; Tulumello and Allegretti 2021; Rossi 2022). Reforms of spatial planning systems took place across crisis-ridden countries under the strain of European institutions and revolutionised territorial governance to the point that literature points to Southern Europe as a prototype of urban neoliberalisation (Tulumello et al. 2020). A peculiar trait of the touristic transformation affecting the cities of the Italian South is that its core is the everyday life of the popular classes living in the historic areas, which appears authentic and folkloric to the external gaze of tourists and investors and forms the backbone of value extraction. The practices, symbols and imaginary informing this life are commodified so that urban poverty does not hamper capitalist accumulation but rather serves it.

The touristic transformation of historic areas based on exploiting the lives of the marginalised is not a new phenomenon. An attitude of "strategic self-orientalism" – an opportunistic self-folklorisation to achieve economic profit – has been adopted by the ruling classes in many cases of popular neighbourhoods being exoticised and sold for their supposed authenticity (Umbach and Wishnoff 2008). What is specific to the Italian scenario is how this process intertwines with the "Southern Question" – the structural imbalance between the North and the South of the country that has been fabricated, both economically and symbolically, ever since national unification. The otherness of the Italian *Mezzogiorno* vis-à-vis the progressed and modern North is not only a discursive order but also a material arrangement of socio-economic disparities produced and reproduced at different moments in national history. Jane Schneider resumed this trajectory of internal racialisation and the asymmetry of power relations it has fostered with the formula of "Orientalism in one country" (Schneider 1998). The Italian South as a margin of capitalist modernity has been created and recreated at every historical juncture of crisis – that is, at every moment of restructuring of the capitalist system – by an ever-renewed interweaving of discursive regimes, public policies and cultural representations to which intellectuals, the political class, institutions and all those subjects contribute who, to use Gramscian vocabulary, create hegemony, that is, an organisation of consensus through which the dominant classes exercise control over the dominated (Forgacs 2014).

Reading the history of modern capitalism from the perspective of the Italian South reveals how, at each moment of capitalist transformation, Southern societies and economies underwent a restructuring that has taken place to perpetuate the otherness of the *Mezzogiorno*.[9] In the post-2008 crisis phase, the otherness of the Italian South has moved from being an obstacle to modernisation – a hurdle to be absorbed into the logic of capitalist progress – to being one of the very targets of accumulation. The transformation of Southern alterity into a trigger for value extraction has occurred through a combination of discourses, policies, laws and cultural representations perpetuating the otherness – vis-à-vis modernity, development, progress – of Southern cities and their populations.

If the otherness of the South is the spirit of Italian capitalism, then the touristic transformation of Southern Italian cities, which proceeds not despite but thanks to the state of socioeconomic exclusion of their popular classes, is no exception to this pattern (Pecile 2020). In cities like Naples and Palermo, where people living in poverty have historically lived in the central areas since the past century, the touristic restructuring has implied a reorganisation of the governance of urban poverty, which has not been necessarily made invisible – pushed to the peripheries – but rather orientalised – staged in *ad hoc* spaces. For popular areas to become tourist destinations, poverty does not have to be hidden: it has to be represented, performed and even parodied. Exhibiting poverty in this way is, after all, consistent with the unique combination of workfare and welfare through which the poor are governed in neoliberal contexts: assistance to them is provided through their forced entry into the labour cycle, one way or another. The poor are produced as subjects through policies and legal rules adopted at all levels of government (Sferrazza Papa 2016). This process is not a sign of the state's withdrawal but of a Janus-faced "centaur state", liberal towards the upper classes and paternalistic towards the poor (Wacquant 2009).

9 The economic boom of the 1950s and 1960s is another phase of restructuring of Italian capitalism that exacerbated the North-South divide and would not have been possible without the exploitation of southern migrants' cheap labour force in the factories of the North. A brilliant analysis of this moment is provided by Paul Ginsborg (1990).

In sum, the trajectory of the commons in Palermo is a litmus test for understanding how the neoliberal restructuring of the Italian South has proceeded in the 2010s. Capitalism in the Italian South thrives not despite but by virtue of the presence of a political society that does not fit into the parameters of civil society. It is the political society's everyday life that allows these cities to become tourist economies and accumulation to continue in new forms. However, this paradox – the poor's lives are the object of value extraction, yet they are in danger of being wiped out by the touristic reconfiguration – undermines the sustainability of livelihoods in the Italian South. Without robust mechanisms for redistributing the wealth generated by tourism to the people who create value, this model promises to be either short-lived or to lead to an unbearable increase in inequalities. In the next chapter, I will suggest that law – a tactic resort to legal technique – could be a powerful tool for urban movements to resist the disruption caused by new extractive processes.

References

Agamben, Giorgio. 1990. *La comunità che viene*. Turin: Bollati Boringhieri.

Baptista, Idalina. 2013. The Travels of Critiques of Neoliberalism: Urban Experiences from the "Borderlands". *Urban Geography* 34(5): 590–611.

Belik, Laura. 2015. Urban Commons and Democracy. In Bologna. http://hdl.handle.net/10535/9962.

Bourdieu, Pierre. 1989. Social Space and Symbolic Power. *Sociological Theory* 7(1): 14–25.

Brenner, Neil, Jamie Peck and Nik Theodore. 2013. Neoliberal Urbanism: Cities and the Rule of Markets. In *The New Blackwell Companion to the City*, Gary Bridge and Sophie Watson (Eds). Oxford: Blackwell, pp. 15–23.

Brown, Wendy. 2015. *Undoing the Demos: Neoliberalism's Stealth Revolution*. New York: Zone Books.

Bürgisser, Reto and Donato Di Carlo. 2023. Blessing or Curse? The Rise of Tourism-Led Growth in Europe's Southern Periphery. *JCMS: Journal of Common Market Studies* 61(1): 236–258.

Butler, Judith. 2004. *Undoing Gender*. New York: Routledge.

Caffentzis, George and Silvia Federici. 2014. Commons against and beyond Capitalism. *Community Development Journal* 49: 92–105.

Calzada, Igor. 2020. Seeing Tourism Transformations in Europe through Algorithmic, Techno-Political and City-Regional Lenses. In *Transforming Tourism: Regional Perspectives on a Global Phenomenon*, Coppieters and Ezkerraberri Foundations (Eds). Brussels: Centre Maurits Coppieters CMC, pp. 74–89.

Clement, Floriane, Wendy Harcourt, Deepa Joshi and Chizu Sato. 2019. Feminist Political Ecologies of the Commons and Commoning (Editorial to the Special Feature). *International Journal of the Commons* 13(1): 1.

Cooper, Davina. 2007. Opening up Ownership: Community Belonging, Belongings, and the Productive Life of Property. *Law & Social Inquiry* 32(3): 625–664.

Cress, Daniel M. and David A. Snow. 1996. Mobilization at the Margins: Resources, Benefactors, and the Viability of Homeless Social Movement Organizations. *American Sociological Review* 61(6): 1089–1109.

Dardot, Pierre and Christian Laval. 2014. *The New Way of the World: On Neo-Liberal Society*. London: Verso Books.

Davies, Margaret. 2012. Persons, Property, and Community. *Feminists@law* 2(2).

De Angelis, Massimo. 2010. The Production of the Commons and the "Explosion" of the Middle Class. *Antipode* 42(4): 954–977.

Del Romero Renau, Luis. 2018. Touristification, Sharing Economies and the New Geography of Urban Conflicts. *Urban Science* 2(4): 104.

De Soto, Hernando. 1989. *The Other Path: The Invisible Revolution in the Third World*. New York: Harper and Row.

Esposito, Roberto. 1998. *Communitas: origine e destino della comunità*. Turin: Einaudi.

Esquirol, Jorge. 2017. Formalizing Property in Latin America. In *Comparative Property Law Perspectives. Research Handbooks in Comparative Law Series*, Michele Graziadei and Lionel Smith (Eds). Edward Elgar Publishing, pp. 333–354.

Federici, Silvia. 2010. Feminism and the Politics of the Commons. In *Uses of a Whirlwind: Movement, Movements, and Contemporary Radical Currents in the United States*, Team Colors Collective (Ed.). Oakland, CA: AK Press, pp. 283–294.

Forgacs, David. 2014. *Italy's Margins: Social Exclusion and Nation Formation since 1861*. Cambridge: Cambridge University Press.

Foucault, Michel. 1996. *Foucault Live: Interviews, 1961–84*, Sylvère Lotringer (Ed.). South Pasadena, CA: Semiotext.

Gago, Verónica. 2017. *Neoliberalism from Below: Popular Pragmatics and Baroque Economies*. Durham, NC: Duke University Press.

Galeota Lanza, Giovanna and Mattia De Martino. 2022. Urban Housing Inequity: Housing Deprivation and Social Response in the City of Naples. *Sustainability* 14(3): 1047.

Gargiulo, Enrico and Adriano Cirulli. 2016. Gli spazi occupati a Napoli. Informalità, trasformazioni urbane e discorsi sui "beni comuni". In *Società, Economia e Spazio a Napoli. Esplorazioni e Riflessioni*, Working Papers, Gabriella Punziano (Ed.). L'Aquila: GSSI Social Sciences, pp. 85–96.

Ginsborg, Paul. 1990. *A History of Contemporary Italy: 1943–1980*. London: Penguin.

Hardt, Michael and Antonio Negri. 2009. *Commonwealth*. Cambridge, MA: Harvard University Press.

Hardt, Michael and Antonio Negri. 2017. *Assembly*. New York: Oxford University Press.

Harrison, Oliver. 2014. *Revolutionary Subjectivity in Post-Marxist Thought: Laclau, Negri, Badiou*. Farnham: Ashgate.

Harvey, David. 1989. From Managerialism to Entrepreneurialism: The Transformation in Urban Governance in Late Capitalism. *Geografiska Annaler. Series B, Human Geography* 71(1): 3–17.

Kaika, Maria. 2017. Between Compassion and Racism: How the Biopolitics of Neoliberal Welfare Turns Citizens into Affective "Idiots". *European Planning Studies* 25(8): 1275–1291.

Laclau, Ernesto. 2005. *On Populist Reason*. London: Verso.

Linebaugh, Peter. 2008. *The Magna Carta Manifesto: Liberties and Commons for All*. Berkeley, CA: University of California Press.

Mattei, Ugo. 2011. *Beni Comuni: Un Manifesto*. Bari: Laterza.

Mendes, Luís. 2018.'Tourism Gentrification in Lisbon: The Panacea of Touristification as a Scenario of Post-Capitalist Crisis. In *Crisis, Austerity, and Transformation: How Disciplinary Neoliberalism Is Changing Portugal*. Lanham, MD: Lexington Books, pp. 25–46.

Mezzadra, Sandro. 2023. Presentazione dell'edizione italiana. In *Neoliberalismo Dal Basso. Economie Barocche e Pragmatica Popolare*, Verónica Gago (Ed.). Naples: Tamu Edizioni.

Mudu, Pierpaolo. 2015. At the Intersection of Anarchists and Autonomists: Autogestioni and Centri Sociali. *ACME: An International Journal for Critical Geographies* 11(3): 413–438.

Nancy, Jean-Luc. 1983. *La Communauté Désœuvrée*. Paris: Christian Bourgois.

NeJaime, Douglas. 2013. Constitutional Change, Courts, and Social Movements. *Michigan Law Review* 111(6):877–902.

Ong, Aihwa. 2006. *Neoliberalism as Exception. Mutations in Citizenship and Sovereignty*. Durham, NC: Duke University Press.

Pecile, Veronica. 2022. Between Urban Commons and Touristification: Radical and Conservative Uses of the Law in Post-Austerity Southern Italy. *City* 26(5–6): 998–1011.

Peck, Jamie. 2012. Austerity Urbanism. *City* 16(6): 626–655.

Piven, Frances Fox and Richard A. Cloward. 1977. *Poor People's Movements: Why They Succeed, How They Fail*. New York: Pantheon Books.

Rolnik, Raquel. 2019. *Urban Warfare. Housing under the Empire of Finance*. London: Verso.

Rossi, Ugo. 2022. The Existential Threat of Urban Social Extractivism: Urban Revival and the Extinction Crisis in the European South. *Antipode* 54(3): 892–913.

Ruggiero, Vincenzo. 2000. New Social Movements and the "Centri Sociali" in Milan. *The Sociological Review* 48(2): 167–185.

Sabariego, Jesús. 2022. The Impact of Social Movements on Public Awareness of a Commons-Based Democracy: Technopolitical Approaches of Portuguese and Spanish Recent Global Social Movements. In *Social Welfare Issues in Southern Europe*. London: Routledge.

Sacco, Pier Luigi, Maria Tartari, Guido Ferilli and Giorgio Tavano Blessi. 2019. Gentrification as Space Domestication. The High Line Art Case. *Urban Geography* 40(4): 529–554.

Saitta, Pietro. 2019. Misure anti accattonaggio, il sociologo: "Cara assessora Musolino, La realtà è più complessa di un'ordinanza". *Lettera Emme*. www.letteraemme.it/2019/07/22/misure-anti-accattonaggio-il-sociologo-cara-assessora-musolino-la-realta-e-piu-complessa-di-unordinanza.

Sassatelli, Roberta, Marco Santoro and Giovanni Semi. 2015. *Fronteggiare la crisi: come cambia lo stile di vita del ceto medio*. Bologna: Il Mulino.

Sato, Chizu and Jozelin María Soto Alarcón. 2019. Toward a Postcapitalist Feminist Political Ecology' Approach to the Commons and Commoning. *International Journal of the Commons* 13(1): 36.

Schneider, Jane. 1998. Introduction: The Dynamics of Neo-Orientalism in Italy (1848–1995). In *Italy's 'Southern Question'. Orientalism in One Country*, Jane Schneider (Ed.). Oxford and New York: Berg, pp. 1–23.

Sequera, Jorge and Jordi Nofre. 2018. Shaken, Not Stirred: New Debates on Touristification and the Limits of Gentrification. *City* 22(5–6): 843–855.

Sferrazza Papa, Ernesto. 2016. Beati e pezzenti: il governo spaziale della povertà. In *I poveri, la povertà, Quaderni materialisti*. Udine: Mimesis, pp. 107–120.

Spanò, Michele. 2013. Negoziare. Sulla governamentalità neoliberale. In *Neoliberalismo come eccezione. Cittadinanza e sovranità in mutazione*, Michele Spanò (Ed.). Lucca: VoLo publisher, pp. 9–22.

Stein, Samuel. 2020. Tourism: An Ideology and an Accumulation Strategy. In *City Killers – A Critique of Tourism*, L. Tozzi (Ed.). Rome: Libria/Campo, pp. 25–32.

Tulumello, Simone. 2016. Reconsidering Neoliberal Urban Planning in Times of Crisis: Urban Regeneration Policy in a "Dense" Space in Lisbon. *Urban Geography* 37(1): 117–140.

Tulumello, Simone. 2019. Struggling Against Entrenched Austerity. From the Housing Crisis toward Social Movements for Housing in Post-Crisis Lisbon and Portugal. *Urban Resilience, Changing Economy and Social Trends. Coping with socio-economic consequences of the crisis in Athens, Greece.* Hannover: Leibniz Universität Hannover, Institut für Umweltplanung, pp. 61–79.

Tulumello, Simone and Giovanni Allegretti. 2021. Articulating Urban Change in Southern Europe: Gentrification, Touristification and Financialisation in Mouraria, Lisbon. *European urban and regional studies* 28(2): 111–132.

Tulumello, Simone, Giancarlo Cotella and Frank Othengrafen. 2020. Spatial Planning and Territorial Governance in Southern Europe between Economic Crisis and Austerity Policies. *International Planning Studies* 25(1): 72–87.

Umbach, Greg ('Fritz') and Dan Wishnoff. 2008. Strategic Self-Orientalism: Urban Planning Policies and the Shaping of New York City's Chinatown, 1950–2005. *Journal of Planning History* 7(3): 214–238.

Vasudevan, Alexander. 2015. The Autonomous City: Towards a Critical Geography of Occupation. *Progress in Human Geography* 39(3): 316–337.

Wacquant, Loïc. 2009. *Punishing the Poor. The Neoliberal Government of Social Insecurity*. Durham, NC: Duke University Press.

Policy and legal sources

Comune di Palermo. 2019. 'Regolamento dei mercati generali' (Deliberazione di Consiglio Comunale n. 147 del 10/04/2019).

Ministero della Cultura. 2018. 'Piano Operativo Cultura e Turismo 2014–2020'. SG MiC – Programmazione e Attuazione Strategica Nazionale e Comunitaria.

Chapter 3

What does property have to do with this? Mistrust towards law and ways out of it

Introduction

A widespread mistrust about the use of the law to realise emancipatory political projects pervades critical theory and has had an impact on the practice of social movements, including the mobilisations for the commons. While activists may use legal tactics for counter-hegemonic purposes, as was the case in part of the Italian movement for the commons in the 2010s, what persists is a specific conception of law as one of the main "master's tools", to use Audre Lorde's formulation – an instrument that is in the hands of the ruling classes and that can at best bring about reforms, but ultimately cannot change existing power relations and patterns of inequality.[1] In this view, law is often equated with criminal law, intertwined with an unspecified notion of power, a tool reproducing domination through its institutional mechanisms.

Of course, there is a genealogy of the relationship between social movements and the use of law that goes in a completely different direction and shows what can happen when the two come together. In Western societies, the civil rights era was a crucial moment in challenging the mistrust about emancipatory uses of law. Activists made extensively use of courtrooms, animated by the conviction that legal reform could indeed contribute to structural change. The renewed attitude towards law implied an original combination of grassroots political practices and legal advocacy, resulting in what social movements scholars have called a hybrid law and organising approach (Cummings and Eagly 2001). Movements came to recognise that law is not necessarily a master's tool, but rather a technique that anyone could use to make their claims, a "machine of abstraction" that produces and reproduces social reality (Spanò 2015: 89) and the political opportunities that the use of such a machine offers.

Scholarship focusing on the Italian struggle for the commons in the 2010s has enthusiastically pointed to the movement's use of legal tools in several

1 The expression is taken from the title of Audre Lorde's collection of essays, *The Master's Tools Won't Dismantle the Master's House* (Lorde 2018).

DOI: 10.4324/9781003335320-4

instances – the Valle Theatre being the most glaring example – and how this was a means of achieving social justice and wealth redistribution in the post-2008 phase when the privatisation processes targeting resources and services triggered a wave of mobilisations worldwide. Critical legal scholars have focused on the uses of law made by activists to claim a right to collective use and access to spaces that ensure the exercise of fundamental rights, following the Rodotà Commission's definition of the commons. These uses of law included access to courts, the creation of institutional arrangements for the collective management of spaces and the recourse to EU legal mechanisms for public participation (Bailey and Mattei 2013). Overall, it has been highlighted how the movement for the commons has engaged in a contestation "on the field" against the absolute and individualistic vision of property dominant in the Western legal tradition (Marella 2017).

Despite these approaches, scepticism persists in theoretical discussions and among social movements about the potential of resorting to law to bring about systemic change beyond reformist objectives. This mistrust contributes to making mobilisations vulnerable to attempts at co-optation, which are also conducted through legal means, as the story of the Southern Italian commons shows. Abandoning the possibility of using law favours the uses of legal tools by other groups and, in the case of the commons, leaves room for a governmental, top-down legal concept of the commons to become hegemonic.

However, it is important to escape paternalistic visions of what power is – which would lead us to think that co-optation means the total neutralisation of the movement's demands. As it turned out, the entanglement of the commons into co-opting dynamics was a complex process, in which groups reclaiming them played an active role, and did not imply the suppression of radical claims to urban space. Indeed, resistance can emerge and flow through the very cracks, the interstices left open by the established legal regime that enshrines the rules of use and access to urban space. A wide range of legal tools are available here and now, in the existing legal systems, to be used by groups seeking to protect the property interests of the popular classes. For social movements, using these tools means changing existing property arrangements and re-signifying what property is.

This chapter is divided into three parts. In the first one, I explore some of the key theoretical roots of the scepticism about law as a tool for achieving structural change. I focus on how the possibility of using legal tools for radical purposes is dismissed by some important strands of critical theory, and what set of assumptions about the relationship between the legal and the political underpins this mistrust. As I will argue, this "suspicious mind" towards law is based on some specific interpretations of the Marxist and Foucaldian thought, in which the distinction between law and power is erased and law is reduced to its repressive function. In the second section, I consider some possible remedies to this anti-legal attitude that are available in the theoretical and the technical-legal sphere. With regard to the former, I examine the thesis, developed in the traditions of legal realism and critical legal studies, that law is inherently indeterminate and open to different political projects – a ductility that makes it suitable to serve as a battleground for advancing social conflict. Adopting a critical legal perspective means acknowledging that law structures social reality so that there is no outside of it; and yet, the fact that it organises all of social and economic life – that it constantly regulates it, even when it does not explicitly do so – is empowering for social movements. Rethinking law, and especially property law, from the margins is an urgent theoretical and political project in times of growing socioeconomic inequalities, in order to protect the popular classes whose lives are the target of value extraction. On the technical-legal level, I present a series of legal "tricks" that social movements have used in recent years to defend the property interests of the city's most marginalised residents and to challenge dominant notions of property. These legal ruses illustrate the extent to which a pragmatic recourse to law offers opportunities to resist patterns of domination and exploitation. In the third and final section, I turn to the ongoing extension of legal personhood to non-human entities, such as the natural world, future life and even non-life, as a promising area for finding legal tools to represent a not-one, assembled subject – in other words, to institute the collective.

The "anti-law" stance in critical theory

The main arguments of the anti-law stance to the test of the Southern Italian commons

Various strands of contemporary critical theory are skeptical about the potential of law to address the socioeconomic structures that reproduce patterns of inequality. According to this stance, it would be an intrinsic quality of law and its operations to formalise existing relations of domination. What is then called for is a political practice that is completely liberated from legal relations, in an alleged realm outside law. Some in this scholarly debate have warned of the danger of what they see as a legalist drift in politics. An important reason why social struggles are only partially successful, it is argued, is that the language of law is increasingly replacing and hollowing out the one of politics. Several examples are provided to support of this thesis: the widespread recourse to affirmative action would dilute the claims of anti-racist protests; discourses promoting formal equality would undermine the quest for substantive equality pursued by LGBTQI+ communities; in short, any decision made by activists to enter the legal arena would end up weakening the radical potential of their demands and accelerate the path leading to their political neutralisation. Law would thus act as a blinder – obscuring the material reality of power relations and reinforcing existing structures of oppression through its universalist language (Xifaras 2018). The "legalistic turn" in left-wing political projects would actually reinforce the very patterns of inequality that social struggles seek to challenge (Brown and Halley 2002). The only way to escape the formal discourse of rights and the rhetoric of the rule of law would be to escape law altogether, to avoid considering it as a realm in which any claims can be made.

Such arguments imply a particular conception of what law is, and of the relationship between law and politics, which is questionable for at least three reasons. First, these approaches seem to equate law with the arithmetical sum of the existing legal rules, especially those that emanate from the state level. What this view overlooks is how the law functions as a field – as a dynamic realm in which different actors expressing different positions of power co-exist and compete for the right to determine the content of legal rules, what Bourdieu famously defined as the "juridical field" (Bourdieu 1987: 817). Second, such a perspective reduces law to its repressive function, epitomised by criminal law, and regards it as the violent end of power. The adoption of such a perspective by social movements is understandable and is often linked to a lived experience of harsh state repression against social protest. In the Italian context, for example, the tools of penal law have been used extensively by the judiciary power against activists reclaiming the commons to oppose the privatisation of natural resources, as demonstrated by the criminalisation suffered by the "No TAV" movement in Piedmont's Susa Valley (Engel-Di Mauro 2013). A third controversial point of the arguments pointing to a legalistic drift of politics in Western societies is the underlying assumption that a sharp separation exists between the realm of law and that of politics. While certainly being a useful analytical tool, this demarcation does not take into account the contamination that constantly occurs between the two and that can only be detected by adopting an ethnographic approach to law and focusing on the production of normativities from the grassroots. Adopting such a perspective this method reveals how the law/politics separation can hardly be drawn when considering cases of legal and political negotiation, how legal reform can take place under political pressure, as well as the extent to which political practice can be boosted by legislative progress.

This vision of law leads to a narrow understanding of its forms, such as property. Important voices in critical theory conceptualise the commons as a radical political horizon that would realise a complete overcoming of law. In *Assembly*, the third chapter of the trilogy that includes *Empire* and *Commonwealth*, Hardt and Negri focus on the radical potential of the contemporary social movements that are leaderless, namely characterised by a dispersed or even non-existent leadership. The thesis is that where there are the commons, there is no property, and vice versa: the commons are "a fundamentally different means of organising the use and management of wealth" and because of this non-proprietary nature, they are the negative of property (Hardt and Negri 2017: 97). When activists call for legal reforms to change property, the result is a reaffirmation of the state's power and a strengthening of its sovereignty at a time when it is in crisis. Movements should rather focus on dismantling state power and sovereignty, and this can only be done by refusing to use law as a tactic for emancipatory ends: "legal projects to reform property and limit its power have certainly had beneficial effects but now we need to finally take the leap beyond" (ibid.: 120). The "leap beyond" is an image used to describe the steps by which activists should finally succeed in doing without law in their quest for a post-capitalist order.

The threefold conception of law underlying this thesis – law as the sum of existing legal rules, law as the violent end of power, law as separated from politics – is dismissed quite radically by the story of the Southern Italian commons. First, the interaction between the different subjects involved in the government of urban space takes place in a realm that is also a legal field–a space in which legal rules are available for negotiation, even if not all the subjects involved participate in this process from the same power position. Second, the kind of legal tools at stake in this negotiation belong to private law, i.e., to a side of law that is descriptive rather than punitive, that gives definitions – of what property is – rather than prohibitions. Thirdly, the Southern Italian commons seem to prove that there is a constant exchange of languages and practices between "the legal" and "the political", which deeply questions the validity of a "law vs. politics" analytical framework.

The intellectual roots of the anti-law attitude

The scepticism of critical theory towards law has illustrious ancestors. Indeed, the roots of this suspicion can be traced in situated readings of some of the foundational thinkers of Western modern thought. It may then be useful to draw an intellectual genealogy of this attitude, albeit an inevitably partial one. Beginning to unravel the theoretical underpinnings of this mistrust can help to rethink the relationship between law and politics and open up possibilities for radical uses of law beyond its repressive function.[2] The first root of the anti-law stance in critical theory is Marx, and in particular the debate about the role of law that runs through his work. It has been argued that because Marxist analysis is concerned with the economic structure and power relations that permeate society, there is no proper Marxist theory of law (Guastini 1980: 14). However, Marx pays considerable attention to law in the form of property relations and how they play out in capitalist systems (Collins 1996: 9). For instance, in his critique of Hegel's philosophy of law, Marx states that legal relations are built upon material relations, i.e., relations of production. The sum of these forms the economic structure of society, that is, the real foundation on which the political and legal superstructures are built (Marx 1859). Law

2 I owe to Lorenzo Coccoli's intervention at the Summer School of the Department of Law at the University of Perugia in 2019 the hints for this attempt to sketch a genealogy of anti-juridism in critical theory.

and politics are then conceived as separate fields both existing at the level of the superstructure. Law secures existing economic relations through the penal tool, hence the importance of criminal law as a stabilising instrument in capitalist societies. As a consequence of this focus on the criminal side of law, which is nevertheless only part of Marx's interest in law, Marxist thought deals with law rather marginally: what is crucial for the distribution of wealth are the relations of production between a capitalist class, which owns the means of production, and a proletariat, which does not. The fact that these relations take a legal form is merely a reflection of the underlying material conditions (Kennedy 1991: 90).[3]

A second basis for the scepticism of critical theory about using law as an emancipatory tool can be found in the poststructuralist debate drawing on the work of Foucault, in particular two texts by the French philosopher. The first one is *The Will to Knowledge*, in which Foucault argues that in order to construct an analytics of power relations, one must go beyond "the juridico-discursive representation of power", since "we have been engaged for centuries in a type of society in which the juridical is increasingly incapable of coding power, of serving it as its system of representation" (Foucault 1998: 89). Power cannot be reduced to its juridico-discursive representation, Foucault suggests, because then it is only a prohibitive power, based on the formulation of a ban, and the other sides of power are neglected as a result. Second, in *Discipline and Punish* the concept of discipline is introduced as a kind of counter-model to law, with disciplinary regimes constituting a distinct, more sophisticated realm than that ruled by law. Here, Foucault's equation seems to be between law and the sovereign's legislation, more specifically the ban (Foucault 1977).

However, Foucault' reflections on law are richer and more nuanced than this emphasis on its prohibitive and disciplinary sides would suggest. Elsewhere in his work, law and power are not conflated and the idea of (repressive) power as essential to legal rules is rejected. This stance is clear in one of the passages outlining the genealogical method: humanity would be far from progressing to the point where the rule of law substitutes warfare and would proceed nonlinearly, through a series of interpretations of each legal rule, which in itself has "no essential meaning" and is instead used "to impose a direction, to bend it to a new will, to force its participation in a different game" (Foucault 1984: 86).

3 A significant exception to this approach towards law in Marxist thought is Pashukanis's critique of law and his thesis of the legal form as the foundation of the capitalist system. In an open polemic against the American legal realists of his own time, Pashukanis rejects the claim that law is neutral and that its forms, such as property, can be used for emancipatory and social purposes. For the Soviet jurist, modern legal forms are not neutral and open to being put at the service of different political projects but are intrinsic to the historical development of the bourgeois society. What is more, for Pashukanis, the legal form is shaped just like the commodity form. Law thus belongs to the structure, not the superstructure, and revolution implies its total extinction (Pashukanis 1987).

This layered conception of the relationship between law and power also emerges from Foucault's reflections on governmentality, which he famously defines as "the ensemble formed by institutions, procedures, analyses and reflections, calculations, and tactics that allow the exercise of this very specific, albeit very complex, power that has the population as its target, political economy as its major form of knowledge, and apparatuses of security as its essential technical instrument" (Foucault 2009: 144).

In sum, the tendency to conflate power with law, and law with its repressive dimension, stems from some situated readings of Marx's and Foucault's thought. On this basis, some critical scholarship concludes that the patterns of domination at work in society are embedded in legal institutions and that emancipation can only be achieved in a sphere outside the legal field (Xifaras 2018). As I will explain, legal realism and critical legal studies provide insights not only for rethinking law as politics all the way down, but also for finding tools within the existing legal framework that allow for reconceiving legal forms, and property in particular, as an emancipatory political project.

Rethinking property as an emancipatory project

The perspective of the critical legal studies: law as politics all the way down

In the 1970s, a movement emerged among North American scholars who intended to recover and renew the tradition of legal realism and offer law school students a radically different education. Back in the 1930s, legal realists had developed their ideas in opposition to the tradition of formalism that was predominant at that time. Whereas for formalists, law was an inherently consistent set of norms – a complete system that does not allow for gaps or indeterminate points in its pattern – realists thought that the study of law had to start from what judges "actually do" – on how legal rules are applied in single cases and how courts make their decisions (Shiner 1995). Because each rule has its exceptions and indeterminacies, realists argued, its application to concrete circumstances can never be univocally determined a priori (Blank and Rosen-Zvi 2010).

In concrete terms, to argue that law is indeterminate means to claim that its tools can be used to realise different political projects. Even if in the history of modern capitalist societies these tools have mainly been used to enact domination and exploitation and preserve the interests of the dominant classes, critical legal scholars argue, law can be used to redistribute wealth and resources in society: as David Kennedy puts it, "we can read in legal norms and institutional arrangements both sediment of past struggle and the tools available for new projects (Kennedy 2016: 171). Law is "at least partially responsible for the outcome of every distributive conflict between classes" (Kennedy 1991: 331) and from such a perspective, refusing to use law altogether would not be politically advantageous for movements: "because it distributes, law has value for people in struggle, and is often also at stake in conflict" (ibid.: 177).

Articulating social conflict in legal terms also means liberating legal concepts of an allegedly immutable essence. When it comes to property, figures such as Hohfeld and Hale conceived it as something inherently coercive but also relational – an intuition first introduced by Roman lawyers and then developed by social legal thought at the end of the nineteenth century (di Robilant 2023). Critical legal studies went one step ahead by arguing that property and all legal forms are "thicker" than conventional legal thinking would let us think because they include a broad set of non-legal contents which are political, social, and even moral. This non-legal character of legal concepts is not a marginal element and makes law available to be used "as the scene of conflict, mediated and administered through the law's allocation of wealth and power" (Schlag 2015: 233).

Critical theory focusing on the commons and social movements reclaiming them would greatly benefit from the hints provided by critical legal studies. What could be especially useful is the distinction between legal forms – that remain largely indifferent to social contents, exist on an abstract plan and can be studied through a history of institutions – and legal practices – the contingent situations in which these forms shape reality. This distinction is not a purely theoretical matter but is crucial to alter and complicate the relation between law and politics as it is theorised by critical theory and experienced by activists. The realm of legal practices, which we might also call the legal field, "has to do with ways and standards which will prevail in the pinch of challenge, with rights and the acquisition of rights which have teeth, with liberties and powers whose exercise can be made to stand up under attack" (Llewellyn 1940: 1364).

Ownership for the non-owners: protecting the property interests of the marginalised

At this point, we might wonder which legal tools are available here and now, in the existing legal system, to redistribute rights, liberties and powers to the most marginalised inhabitants of the city. In other words, we may ask through which arrangements it is possible to protect the property interests of the urban poor whose life provides the core for new modes of value extraction. The suggestion is to turn to the relational core of property, a dynamic in which a set of subjects and groups are involved in different ways, not only the owners but also a plethora of users, passers-by and "have-nots" who have a variety of interests towards the concerned thing or space. Adopting this view has two implications: first, to recognise the conflict that can result from the co-existence of multiple and overlapping property interests over the same thing or space; second, to illuminate a set of property claims that would otherwise remain invisible and dismissed because they "do not look like property to us, and we have tended to ignore them" (Rose 1998: 142).

In other terms, what often lies behind conflicts for urban space – for deciding how it should be used and accessed – are clashes between different property interests and regimes. In a schematic way, there is on one side a public-private property regime, produced and sustained by a coalition of state and market subject-owners, but there is also a grassroots common property regime that expresses the interests of the have-nots (Cuff 1998: 138). From this perspective, practices of occupation, squatting and other uses of space that are deemed illegal are instances of expression of legitimate property rights (Singer 1988).

The point is then to reconceive property from the margins– as a political project able to oppose the "machinery of dispossession" through which an increasingly large number of residents are subjected to eviction and other contemporary forms of dispossession (Rolnik 2019: 4). Adopting a marginal gaze on property allows one to broaden the scope of the analysis to consider not only the practices of the dispossessed and of those who live in material conditions of poverty and deprivation but also of activists, squatters and all "property outlaws" fighting against structures reproducing inequalities (Peñalver and Katyal 2010). Legal arrangements can be fine-tuned to grasp the complexity of all modalities through which the marginalised claim a right to use and access urban space. They allow legally recognising the property interests of all those who do not fit into the parameters of civil society and whose everyday lives imply illegal acts as a way to survive. As Andries van der Walt writes in his study of property transformation and land reforms in South Africa:

> Property law is not exclusively or even primarily about owners and holders of rights, but about those who do not own property and whose lives are shaped and affected by the property holdings of others; those who are required to respect property and who are owned as or through property. In the margins, property law is as deeply concerned with absence of property; no-property; not-property; as it is with property.
>
> (van der Walt 2008: 238)

Rethinking property from the margins is part of rethinking law as a political project for socioeconomic emancipation and wealth redistribution. The margin is a space of radical possibility, an edge of social reality in which communities of resistance are built (hooks 1989). It is a space for legal imagination – to turn law into a tool for reducing the gap between the haves and the have-nots, the oppressors and the oppressed, the centres and the peripheries of power.

What follows is a non-exhaustive list of legal mechanisms for protecting the property interests of the marginalised in contemporary cities, which can be found both in the private and the public law repertoire. While they differ in many respects, what they share is a function of redistribution of wealth and power among those who use and access urban space. These legal tricks are available here and now, in the existing Western legal systems, and show that a legal regime of the commons is already at hand, albeit in a fragmented and inconsistent form. The commons already exist as property and not as its negation.

Community Land Trusts

A legal tool that is paradigmatic of the capacity of the private legal form to accommodate for the commons is the community land trust (CLT), an instrument first introduced during the 1970s. Emerged in response to the need for democratic communal control of land and affordable housing, the CLT came back to the fore after the 2008 economic breakdown when it was adopted by activists struggling with worsening housing crises in North America (Gray 2008; Moore and McKee 2012). To set up a CLT, a group must first gain legal status, for example by establishing a non-profit organisation that promotes access to housing for low-income people who are not owners. The CLT is based on the idea of separating the property title of the land from that of the buildings constructed on it, in order to establish a balance between the interests of the owner and those of the non-owners. The technical trick at the heart of the CLT is to make the group of non-owners the property trustees, which means that they will not fully dispose of it, but they will manage it for the benefit of present and future residents. The simple stratagem of splitting property has the significant effect of removing the real estate built on the land from the dynamics of market speculation it would otherwise be subjected to and that could eventually make it unaffordable for residents.

The CLT has been adopted in hundreds of cases in North America and has subsequently been adopted in some civil law systems, such as the Belgian one (Versele et al. 2013). Its malleable structure allows it to be used not only as an instrument to deal with housing crises but also, more broadly, as a tool for the grassroots government of spaces since its use mitigates the inequalities that can be triggered by urban requalification processes (Vercellone 2016). This is possible because the membership of the CLT remains open and its members are responsible for approving the sale operations related to land, an aspect that guarantees a governance structure committed to democracy and deliberation (di Robilant 2014: 378).

In the Italian context, a proposal of constructing a CLT was advanced by the group occupying the Cavallerizza Reale in Turin, a space declared public heritage by UNESCO that was once used as a stable by the royal family during the Kingdom of Italy. Held for a long time in a state of abandonment, it was occupied in 2014 by a group of activists who reclaimed it as a commons and became one of the city's bulwarks against gentrification. With the support of legal experts who had already been part of the experience of the Rodotà Commission, the occupants drafted a proposal for turning the area of the former Tabasso factory, in the nearby town of Chieri, into a CLT. The municipality expressed scepticism towards this plan and invited the occupants to formulate a plan for regenerating another area, the Cascina Maddalene, into what would have been the first CLT in Italy. Even in this case, the proposal was not realised, with one of the main problems being how to identify the trustee (Cuccia 2019). More recently, though, activists in Turin succeeded in setting up the first Italian CLT, finally introduced through the adoption of a notarial act concerning a private building to be restored and used as social housing unit.

Administrative regulations for the shared government of the commons

As we have seen in Chapter 1 with the regulation for the shared management of the urban commons, public law instruments can create disciplinary effects on urban space when they define the commons and the community taking care of them in legalistic terms. However, there are different ways to frame the commons as a legal concept in public law, and it is also possible to do it in a way that does not tame but amplifies the mobilisations' transformative potential. In the Italian post-crisis setting, the regulation promoted by Labsus based on a governmental notion of the commons and used in hundreds of cities was initially countered by another model adopted in the town of Chieri, later merged into a regulation adopted by the municipality of Turin. At the height of the national struggle for the commons in 2014, a Regulation for the participation in the government and the care of the commons (*Regolamento comunale per la partecipazione nel governo e nella cura dei beni comuni*) was adopted by the municipal council. Unlike the Labsus regulation, which draws on the subsidiarity principle as the main legal basis for the commons, the Chieri regulation is explicitly inspired by the conceptualisation of the commons elaborated by the Rodotà Commission in 2007. Article 1 states that "also in order to protect future generations", the City of Chieri "protects the goods that the community recognises as common, as they are functional to the exercise of people's fundamental rights in their urban and rural ecological context".

Another crucial point of the Chieri regulation is the recognition of informal groups as legitimate subjects for governing the commons. In Article 3, it is established that the "autonomous subjectivities or civic collectivities" are "all subjects, whether individual, associated or otherwise grouped in social formations, including informal ones, who are active in the identification, care and regeneration of specific commons". They, and not the city administration, are the crucial actors in recognising and governing the commons. Article 17 reiterates this idea, stating that "the legal and socioeconomic recognition of urban spaces as commons" is tied to the experimentation with and broadening of participation processes that are anchored in a "community of reference", albeit "informal" in nature. This insistence on informality in the legal text ensures that all residents, regardless of their status, have a right not only to use and access the commons but also to participate in the practices concurring to their self-government (Angiolini 2016). The property interests of the have-nots are thus protected and the commons emerge as a means to rebalance patterns of inequality in favour of the popular classes. This is particularly urgent when the land at stake, either publicly or privately owned, has a high residential value (Mattei and Quarta 2015).

A further important aspect of the Chieri regulation is the link of the commons not with the shared administration between citizens and local state but with the realisation of direct democracy and self-government. Article 20 states that "self-government, accessibility and impartiality in the use of the commons" must be guaranteed and that *beni comuni* are also "spaces in which decision-making practices that determine the conditions of use are exercised". The commons, then, are such not just by virtue of their use but also of how they are managed, namely, through self-government. Article 23, titled "Assembly democracy" (*Democrazia assembleare*), establishes that the only body in charge of making decisions about any project concerning the commons is the self-government assembly (*assemblea di autogestione*). Decisions concerning the use of spaces, the relations with external subjects and financial matters shall all be made by consensus within the Assembly, as set out in Article 24.[4]

Hybrid public/private approaches: civic uses

Another important instrument to legally conceptualise the commons can be found in a tool that, although belonging to the array of techniques of private law, is closer to public law. The civic use (*uso civico*) is a right of collective enjoyment that members of a community can exercise on public or private land for activities such as grazing and hunting (Grossi 1977; Marinelli 2013). Previously, it was relegated to customary law and historically assigned to mountain and inland communities in Northern and Central Italy, which would resort to it in a context of subsistence economy. In recent times, civic uses were recovered by the Italian movement for the commons to legitimise the activists' claims to a collective use and access to urban space. This legal trick was adopted in Naples during the occupation of the ex-Asilo Filangieri in 2012, a sixteenth-century publicly owned palace that the municipality wanted to sell out on the market (Capone 2016). The occupants, backed by the support of legal experts, reclaimed the right to a civic and collective use of this space by invoking precisely the ancient legal institution of *uso civico*. They drafted a regulation which was then submitted to the municipality to provide a legal basis for all the communities occupying spaces in the city with the aim of delivering services to the marginalised, such as self-organised medical clinics

4 The Chieri regulation was amended in 2022 after the municipality agreed to adopt elements of the model of the Labsus regulation. The title of the document was changed by eliminating references to self-government, which have disappeared throughout the text. The concept of autonomy has been kept but appears coupled with another one, that of responsibility. Article 4 of the amended regulation states among the general principles that "the administration values responsibility [...] as a central element in the care, shared administration and regeneration of the commons, as well as a necessary precondition to make collaboration effectively oriented towards the production of useful and measurable results" (Comune di Chieri 2022).

and legal assistance to migrants. The contents of the document were negotiated with the city's administration and led to the adoption of a regulation recognising seven occupied spaces as commons on the legal basis provided by the institution of *uso civico*. The legal text establishes that these spaces are managed by communities in charge of deciding the rules and forms of government through assembly-based methods (Corbisiero 2019). The outcome of this tactic revival of civic uses is, again, the unbundling of property and the distribution of power to marginalised subjects.

Towards the institution of the collective

In this chapter, I discussed the theoretical bases of the scepticism towards the use of law that is adopted by strands of social movements and critical theory and proposed some legal concepts and tools as an antidote to this mistrust. To conclude this reflection, it is worth focusing on a promising realm for further legal experimentation that will be deepened in the final chapter. I am referring to the ongoing debate on the legal representation of non-human entities, which has greatly advanced in recent years with the worsening of the climate crisis (Nash 1989; Voigt 2013), and in more abstract terms on how it is possible to institute the collective (Spanò 2022). In recent times, we have observed a shift from a mainly speculative discussion on this issue to a legal practice of granting legal status to non-humans. These developments occurred decades after Christopher Stone famously proposed that legal rights should be granted to forests, oceans, rivers, and "the natural environment as a whole" (Stone 1972: 456). His proposal was at odds with one of the foundations of modern legal thought, namely, the theory of subjective rights. Elaborated by Savigny, this can be resumed in the idea that each person, and no one else, has legal capacity and this provides the basis for organising social relations (Savigny 1840–49). However, such a construction has been criticised by legal philosophers pointing out how there have always been situations in which rights exist without any subject attached to them, such as in the case of pending inheritance (Orestano 1968; Monterossi 2020).

The rights-based approach to the legal protection of the natural world that has been widespread in recent years translates Stone's proposal in the realm of legal technique. Examples abound in legislation and case law and include the enshrinement of the rights of nature into constitutions (Merino 2018; Tanasescu 2022), the recognition of natural resources and non-human animals as legal subjects (Hermitte 2011; O'Donnell and Talbot-Jones 2018) and the legal acknowledgement of future generations in the name of an intergenerational equity principle (Gosseries 2008). Such transformations also have a significant political impact, as they let new notions of citizenship emerge in the context of the climate crisis (Jasanoff 2010).

These legal advancements have also been met with criticisms by scholars pointing out how the extension of legal personhood to non-human entities, such as the natural world, future life and even non-life does not question the ideological basis of the modern legal subject – a white, male, property-owning being constructed in opposition to a non-white, female, property-less Other that is assimilated to "nature" and made available for exploitation and commodification (Grear 2015; Petersmann 2023). The risk, then, would be reaffirming a relationship between individuals and things that remains utilitarian and extractivist as it has been throughout capitalist modernity. The tool to enact this relationship is the concept of private property that has been predominant in modern legal thought – absolute, individualist and exclusive. The result is a missed opportunity to decentre the modern legal subject and a strengthening of the anthropocentric thinking informing it (Marella 2021).

The point is that decentring the subject is a challenging task to carry out in the domain of legal technique. Modern law seems hardly capable of recognising the ties, networks and webs that transcend the mere individual subject, and it can barely function without constantly referring to the latter as the centre of imputation for all legal relations- a magnetic pole around which interests, rights and duties aggregate. Michele Spanò points out how this aspect of law is not an ideological but a formal one – it has little to do with the ideas and values underpinning modern legal systems but is rather linked to its structural functioning. Individuality is the logic that pervades both private and public law: the former is based on a conception of the individual as an isolated being whose freedom is the one to buy and sell, while the latter is founded on an individual conceived as the atom of the body politic. This dual process of individualisation is the one that defines modern law from its very outset (Spanò 2022). And yet, a genealogical excavation in the forms of Western modern law reveals the existence of legal tools through which the collective can be instituted. As it will be explored in the next chapter, a way to do this is to reconceive property as belonging.

References

Angiolini, Chiara. 2016. Possibilità e limiti dei recenti regolamenti comunali in materia di beni comuni. In *Beni comuni 2.0. Contro-egemonia e nuove istituzioni*, Alessandra Quarta and Michele Spanò (Eds). Milan-Udine: Mimesis, pp. 147–156.

Bailey, Saki and Ugo Mattei. 2013. Social Movements As Constituent Power: The Italian Struggle for The Commons. *Indiana Journal of Global Legal Studies* 20(2): 965–1013.

Blank, Yishai and Issi Rosen-Zvi. 2010. The Spatial Turn in Legal Theory. *HAGAR Studies in Culture, Polity and Identities* 10(1): 37–60.

Bourdieu, Pierre. 1987. The Force of Law: Toward a Sociology of the Juridical Field. *Hastings Law Journal* 38(5): 814–853.

Brown, Wendy and Janet Halley, eds. 2002. *Left Legalism/Left Critique*. Durham, NC: Duke University Press.

Capone, Nicola. 2016. Del diritto d'uso civico e collettivo dei beni destinati al godimento dei diritti fondamentali. *Politica del diritto* 4(XLVIII): 597–636.

Collins, Hugh. 1996. *Marxism and Law*. Oxford: Oxford University Press.

Corbisiero, Fabio. 2019. I beni comuni come antidoto alla turistificazione dei centri storici? Il caso di Santa Fede Liberata a Napoli. Musarò Pierluigi and Piga Bruni Emanuela (Eds). *Scritture migranti*, no. 13: 154–176.

Cuccia, Andrea. 2019. Community Land Trust e beni comuni. Le implicazioni della dimensione comunitaria e i risvolti applicativi in Italia. *LABSUS*.

Cuff, Dana. 1998. Community Property: Enter the Architect or, The Politics of Form. In *Slow Space*, Michael Bell and Sze Tsung Leong (Eds). New York: Monacelli Press.

Cummings, Scott and Ingrid Eagly. 2001. A Critical Reflection on Law and Organizing. *UCLA Law Review* 48: 443–517.

di Robilant, Anna. 2014. Property and Democratic Deliberation: The Numerus Clausus Principle and Democratic Experimentalism in Property Law. *American Journal of Comparative Law* 62(2): 367–416.

di Robilant, Anna. 2023. *The Making of Modern Property: Reinventing Roman Law in Europe and Its Peripheries 1789–1950*. Cambridge, MA: Cambridge University Press.

Engel-Di Mauro, Salvatore. 2013. Introduction to the Symposium: Hints of Post-Capitalist Prefiguration in Val Di Susa (NW Italy). *Capitalism Nature Socialism* 24(2): 7–13.

Foucault, Michel. 1977. *Discipline and Punish: The Birth of the Prison*. New York: Pantheon Books.

Foucault, Michel. 1984. Nietzsche, Genealogy, History. In *The Foucault Reader*, Paul Rabinow (Ed.). New York: Pantheon Books, pp. 76–100.

Foucault, Michel. 1998. *1 The History of Sexuality: The Will to Knowledge*. London: Penguin.

Foucault, Michel. 2009. *Security, Territory, Population: Lectures at the Collège de France 1977–1978*, Michael Senellart, François Ewald and Alessandro Fontana (Eds). London: Palgrave Macmillan.

Gosseries, Axel. 2008. On Future Generations' Future Rights*. *Journal of Political Philosophy* 16(4): 446–474.

Gray, Karen A. 2008. Community Land Trusts in the United States. *Journal of Community Practice* 16(1): 65–78.

Grear, Anna. 2015. Deconstructing Anthropos: A Critical Legal Reflection on "Anthropocentric" Law and Anthropocene "Humanity". *Law and Critique* 26(3): 225–249.

Grossi, Paolo. 1977. *Un altro modo di possedere. L'emersione di forme alternative di proprietà alla coscienza giuridica postunitaria*. Milan: Giuffrè.

Guastini, Riccardo. 1980. *Marxismo e teorie del diritto*. Bologna: Il Mulino.

Hardt, Michael and Antonio Negri. 2017. *Assembly*. New York: Oxford University Press.

Hermitte, Marie-Angèle. 2011. La Nature, Sujet de Droit?. *Annales. Histoire, Sciences Sociales* 66(1): 173–212.

Hohfeld, Wesley Newcomb. 1913. Some Fundamental Legal Conceptions as Applied in Judicial Reasoning. *The Yale Law Journal* 23(1): 16–59.

hooks, bell. 1989. Choosing the Margin as a Space of Radical Openness. *Framework: The Journal of Cinema and Media* 36: 15–23.

Jasanoff, Sheila. 2010. A New Climate for Society. *Theory, Culture & Society* 27(2–3): 233–253.

Kennedy, David. 2016. *A World of Struggle: How Power, Law, and Expertise Shape Global Political Economy*. Princeton, NJ: Princeton University Press.

Kennedy, Duncan. 1991. The Stakes of Law or Hale and Foucault!. *Legal Studies Forum* XV(4): 328–341.

Llewellyn, Karl N. 1940. The Normative, the Legal and the Law-Jobs. *Yale Law Journal* 49: 1355–1400.

Lorde, Audre. 2018. *The Master's Tools Will Never Dismantle the Master's House*. London: Penguin.

Marella, Maria Rosaria. 2017. Queer eye for the straight guy. Sulle possibilità di un'analisi giuridica queer. *Politica del diritto* 3(XLVIII): 383–414.

Marella, Maria Rosaria. 2021. An Anthropology of the Legal Subject: On the Transformation of a Legal Concept. *Osservatorio del diritto civile e commerciale* (1), 71–104.

Marinelli, Fabrizio. 2013. *Gli usi civici*. Milan: Giuffrè.

Marx, Karl. 1859. *A Contribution to the Critique of Political Economy*. Translated by S. W. Ryazanskaya. Moscow: Progress Publishers.

Mattei, Ugo and Alessandra Quarta. 2015. Right to the City or Urban Commoning? Thoughts on the Generative Transformation of Property Law. *The Italian Law Journal* 303(1): 303–325.

Merino, Roger. 2018. Reimagining the Nation-State: Indigenous Peoples and the Making of Plurinationalism in Latin America. *Leiden Journal of International Law* 31(4): 773–792.

Monterossi, Michael W. 2020. *L'orizzonte Intergenerazionale Del Diritto Civile. Tutela, Soggettività, Azione*. Vol. 72. Jura. Temi e problemi del diritto. Pisa: ETS Edizioni.

Moore, Tom and Kim McKee. 2012. Empowering Local Communities? An International Review of Community Land Trusts. *Housing Studies* 27(2): 280–290.

Nash, Roderick Frazier. 1989. *The Rights of Nature: A History of Environmental Ethics*. Madison, WI: University of Wisconsin Press.

O'Donnell, Erin L. and Julia Talbot-Jones. 2018. Creating Legal Rights for Rivers: Lessons from Australia, New Zealand, and India. *Ecology and Society* 23(1).

Orestano, Riccardo. 1968. *Il problema delle persone giuridiche in diritto romano*, Vol. I. Turin: Giappichelli.

Pashukanis, Evgeny. 1987. *Law and Marxism: A General Theory*. London: Pluto Press.

Pecile, Veronica. 2023. Rethinking Legal Time: The Temporal Turn in Socio-Legal Studies. *Oñati Socio-Legal Series* 13(S1): S386–401.

Peñalver, Eduardo and Sonia K. Katyal. 2010. *Property Outlaws: How Squatters, Pirates, and Protesters Improve the Law of Ownership*. New Haven, CT: Yale University Press.

Petersmann, Marie-Catherine. 2023. Life Beyond the Law – From the "Living Constitution" to the "Constitution of the Living". *Zeitschrift Für Ausländisches Öffentliches Recht Und Völkerrecht/Heidelberg Journal of International Law* 82(4): 769–800.

Rolnik, Raquel. 2019. *Urban Warfare. Housing under the Empire of Finance*. Translated by Felipe Hirschhorn. London: Verso.

Rose, C. 1998. The Several Futures of Property: Of Cyberspace and Folk Tales, Emission Trades and Ecosystems. *Minnesota Law Review* 83: 129–182.

Savigny, F. Karl. 1840. *System des Heutigen Römischen Rechts*. Berlin:Veit.

Schlag, Pierre. 2015. How to Do Things with Hohfeld. *Law and Contemporary Problems* 78(185): 185–234.

Shiner, Robert A. 1995. Legal Realism. ed. Robert Audi. *The Cambridge Dictionary of Philosophy*.

Singer, Joseph William. 1988. The Reliance Interest in Property. *Stanford Law Review* 40 (3): 611–751.

Spanò, Michele. 2015. Le parole e le cose (del diritto). In *Il valore delle cose*, Michele Spanò (Ed.). Macerata: Quodlibet, pp. 85–98.

Spanò, Michele. 2020. Perché non rendi poi quel che prometti allor? Tecniche e ideologie della giuridificazione della natura. In *L'istituzione della natura*, Michele Spanò (Ed.). Macerata: Quodlibet, pp. 103–124.

Spanò, Michele. 2022. *Fare il molteplice: Il diritto privato alla prova del comune*. Turin: Rosenberg & Sellier.

Stone, Christopher D. 1972. Should Trees Have Standing? Toward Legal Rights for Natural Objects. *Southern California Law Review* 45: 450–501.

Tanasescu, Mihnea. 2022. *Understanding the Rights of Nature: A Critical Introduction*. Bielefeld: Transcript.

van der Walt, Andries. 2009. *Property in the Margins*. Oxford and Portland, OR: Hart Publishing.

Vercellone, Antonio. 2016. Urban commons e modelli di governo. Il Community Land Trust. In *Beni Comuni 2.0. Contro-egemonia e nuove istituzioni*, Alessandra Quarta and Michele Spanò (Eds). Milan-Udine: Mimesis, pp. 171–184.

Versele, Alexis, Barbara Wauman, Katrien Biesbroeck and Hilde Breesch. 2013. Community Land Trust to Achieve Sustainable Housing in a Working-Class Neighbourhood in Gent (Belgium). In European SPES Conference: Responsibility in Economics. The Legacy of E.F. Schumacher, pp. 249–263.

Voigt, Christina, ed. 2013. *Rule of Law for Nature: New Dimensions and Ideas in Environmental Law*. Cambridge: Cambridge University Press.

Xifaras, Mikhaïl. 2018. The Role of the Law in Critical Theory. The Case of Property and the Commons (As a Commentary on the First Chapter of Negri and Hardt's Commonwealth). In *Critique and Praxis 13/13*. Columbia University.

Legal sources

Comune di Chieri. 2014. 'Regolamento comunale per la partecipazione nel governo e nella cura dei beni comuni' (Deliberazione del Consiglio Comunale n. 105 del 24/11/2014).

Comune di Chieri. 2022. 'Regolamento sulla collaborazione tra cittadini e amministrazione per la cura, la gestione condivisa e la rigenerazione dei beni comuni' (Deliberazione del Consiglio Comunale n. 52 del 30/05/2022).

Chapter 4

Legal forms to the test of the Southern Italian commons

A non-proprietary ownership?

A critical and historical approach to legal forms

In this final chapter, I reconsider the Palermo story of the commons from the viewpoint of legal theory and take it as a cue to rethink and rearticulate some categories central to modern law. Drawing on the observed practices, I sketch a model of legal abstraction constructed on two legal forms: belonging understood as broader than ownership, and things considered not as pre-given, but built through legal technique. The adopted approach is thus at once critical and historical. It is critical because it focuses on the Palermo experience of the commons to ask questions concerning its impact on legal forms; and it is historical in the sense of based on a genealogical approach to legal forms, attentive to their marginal uses, and to law as a technique contributing to the formation of modern societies – a process of abstraction that passes through the concrete acts of institutions. Integrating a genealogical perspective into the critical work is crucial, I believe, to develop critique as Judith Butler suggests – as an exercise in imagining and generating new ways of living in the world instead of a purely destructive and nihilist posture (Butler 2009). This chapter attempts to make such an effort and is a complement to the political-philosophical reflection conducted in Chapter 2 and the critical-legal inquiry carried out in Chapter 3. The focus will be on finding in the trajectory of the Southern Italian commons the elements for an alternative property regime instituting a relationship between individuals and things that departs from possessive individualism and affirms a relation between individuals and things in which use and access are redistributed in favour of the non-owners.

In the first part of the chapter, I will explore the relationship between individuals and things revealed in the Palermo story of the commons and how it can be legally described. To this aim, I retrieve a category that occupies a prior and antecedent place to property if we adopt a genealogical approach to modern legal forms: belonging, or what Roman jurists called *pertinere*. I argue that reading the experience of cultural spaces reclaimed as commons through the theoretical framework offered by the category of *pertinere* (belonging), rather than the narrower one of *possidere* (ownership), allows one to grasp the

DOI: 10.4324/9781003335320-5

complexity of the web of property relations at play that are overlooked by a conventional model of private property.

In the second part, I will draw on the example of the market regularisation in Ballarò in order to reflect on how things are made as such through law. Drawing on the materialist and structuralist approach to legal forms developed by Yan Thomas, I adopt a perspective in which things, such as those reclaimed as commons, do not pre-exist law but are produced by means of legal technique. The focus is then on the use of specific legal arrangements that reinstate a physical market place, namely a localised and regulated portion of the city's territory in which all activities are made visible and subjected to public control. I will ground this construction in the operations of Roman law concerning "things" (*res*), which, as Thomas carefully reconstructed, do not exist "out there", as ontological pre-givens for jurists but are normatively constructed as such through legal procedure (*causa*). Reviving this non-essentialist and non-naturalist approach to things is useful not only to understand the theoretical legal implications of the mobilisations for the commons but also to imagine arrangements that institute the collective in times of economic and ecological crisis.

Having identified belonging as wider than property and things as constructed through legal technique as the central tenets of an abstraction model for rethinking the relation between individuals and things, I will conclude by turning to the Neapolitan experience of the commons in the 2010s. This focus will show how diverse legal tactics were used by the mobilisation of the commons in the Italian South and will clarify how a model of non-proprietary ownership emerges from such practices.

Belonging, or wider than property

Belonging

In the second century, jurist Sextius Pomponius wrote a long comment to the three books of civil law of the jurist Masurius Sabinus. A fragment of this work deals with the topic of belonging and is collected in the Digest, the compendium of legal writings on Roman law compiled four centuries later for the will of Emperor Justinian I. In the fragment D.50.16.181, included in the book *De significatione verborum* ("On the meaning of words"), Pomponius wrote:

> Verbum illud "pertinere" latissime patet: nam et eis rebus petendis aptum est, quae dominii nostri sint, et eis, quas iure aliquo possideamus, quamvis non sint nostri dominii.
>
> The verb to belong has a very wide range of meanings: it applies to things that are our property, but also to things over which we have certain rights, even if they are not our property.
>
> (Watson 1998)

In the sense conventionally adopted in modern legal thought, belonging works as a synonym for owning. It designates the same appropriative relationship between a subject and a thing, but from the point of view of the latter instead of the former: a thing belongs to a subject because the subject owns it, in a perfectly circular relation. Pomponius's fragment allows one to take a step back from this reductionism. It opens up the possibility of considering *pertinere* as something decoupled from *possidere* – as detached from property meant as an exclusive mode of ownership based on the owner's control over the thing.

In other words, a thing can belong to me even though I am not its owner. If I am the usufructuary or a simple user of a thing, then I can claim that it belongs to me, even though the owner is someone else. Belonging and owning reveal themselves as not symmetrical, as they express very different kinds of relationships to things; the former is much broader, richer and accommodating for a variety of political contents than the latter. This point has some subtle implications that go beyond the mere subject-object relation. Belonging alters not only one's relationship with things but also one's whole life as an individual in society. For example, it changes what it means to claim to be a formal citizen and thus to belong to a political community. Belonging will no longer mean being part of a pre-constituted community determined by some essence; instead, the community will be ephemeral, open and determined mainly by the practices through which its members relate to things – by their use of them.

Having clarified the meaning of belonging, let us now return to the Southern Italian commons from which we started. Let us see which forms of relations between individuals and things emerge from the practices analysed and conducted under the label of commons in Palermo. What follows is an attempt to integrate the commons as a floating noun, which was the focus of Chapter 2, with legal content that signifies it. I will turn to the commons as an empty signifier – not anchored in a single legal concept and circulating as a word, as a communicative device – in order to connect it to a legal substance, stable and no longer volatile, that can provide them with autonomous consistency.

The shape(s) of property

The observation of the first group of experiences, the occupation of cultural spaces conducted in the name of the commons, recalls the concept of *pertinere* so far resumed. The Garibaldi Theatre, the Occupied Mediterranean Theatre, the Zisa warehouses, even the Valle Theatre in Rome: in all these cases, relationships developed between persons and spaces in which the goal was neither appropriation nor instrumental use, and what emerged was precisely a dimension of belonging. What was overturned through these practices is the idea of private property as the sign of an original subjective power over things, expressed in the forms of appropriation and exchange (Napoli 2015). In these lived experiences, *pertinere* emerged as a category above *possidere*: the spaces belonged to the users, and this mattered more than the fact that they were owned by someone else. The logical primacy of belonging over ownership is thus justified not only on the philological and historical plan of the Western legal tradition, as Pomponius's fragment proves, but also on a political plan, since what happened to these spaces – the uses that were made of them, the practices that affected them – suspended the power of the conventional concept of property as the owner's unlimited control over a thing or space.

Having clarified that the category of belonging can be useful to designate the mobilisations for the commons, we need to understand more precisely how this concept is helpful in describing, in terms of legal abstraction, what happened in the reclaimed spaces. With Davina Cooper, we may ask: "what kind of belonging is this?" (Cooper 2014: 161). In her work on what she calls everyday utopias – a diverse set of spaces where everyday life is organised in radically diverging ways from conventional social and political structures in the global North – Cooper shows how property is reimagined and re-practiced through experiences of communal living. In these cases, to focus only on the property relations recognised by the state would mean missing much of what is going on: it would imply, for instance, not noticing how, in these places, property and governance are intertwined in attempts at self-government and direct democracy; or how it is not only the users who "make" the space through their use but also vice versa – a community is constituted as such by the relation it maintains to a thing. Cooper deploys belonging as a more appropriate category than property conventionally intended to explore the layers of property relations, between individuals but also between individuals and things, that are at stake in communal experiences. In particular, she points to three variants of belonging for illuminating the complexity of such relations: conventional property, constitutive relationship and proper attachment (Cooper 2014: 161–163).

The first form of belonging identified by Cooper is the one that in modern legal thought is conventionally associated with property. This kind of belonging is often explained in legal theory through the metaphor of the bundle of sticks. According to this image, property is not a monolithic entity but is made up of a set of elements – the sticks – corresponding to various powers and rights held by different actors who have different property interests in the thing. This picture of property as a bundle was famously introduced by Hohfeld and then elaborated by the legal realists. One of its implications is a dimension of malleability: sticks can be added, removed and redistributed among individuals, thus changing the distribution of power and resources (di Robilant 2013). We may see this as an arithmetical view of property, as it were, a kind of "level zero" of belonging. It is what we observe at work in the cultural spaces reclaimed as commons in Palermo and in similar situations in which a place was reclaimed as commons because activists consider it as linked to the fulfilment of a right. The spaces in question belonged to an owner – the public actor – who held the property title but, for a certain amount of time, granted a right of access to the users. This concession was made in a more or less peaceful way, as shown by the eviction attempts made by the police in these spaces, which can be read as moments in which the sticks that make up property were being reshuffled and reassigned in a conflictual way.

A second, more sophisticated form that belonging can assume, defined by Davina Cooper as "less obviously agentic" than the one just described, is constitutive belonging. This refers to a kind of relation between persons and things that is not merely instrumental or based on an opportunistic use of the resource but is instead dynamic and "mutually formative", in the sense that each part involved "takes shape in and through the other" (Cooper 2014: 162). It is the kind of relationship that bound together occupied cultural spaces and the groups reclaiming them as commons in Palermo and elsewhere, and which a vast literature refers to as "commoning" – implying that the commons are the result of a process by which a thing or space is produced, an activity rather than an object, a verb instead of a noun. Adopting this view means that spaces reclaimed as commons belong more to those who use them than to the owners (Linebaugh 2008; Bresnihan and Byrne 2015; Bollier 2020). From this perspective, property law ceases to be mainly about owners and holders of rights and is about the property interests of the have-nots whose lives are shaped by others' property holdings (van der Walt 2009). This is especially true if the latter are negligent or absent in taking care of the space. In this case, the co-constitutive relationship between the thing and the community taking care of it emerges as paramount in determining the destiny of the space, way more than what would be determined by the property title.

A third variant of belonging identified by Cooper is proper attachment, which is related to, but not identical to constitutive belonging. It consists of a relationship of connection and proximity between individuals and things that can also be made counter-hegemonically, that is, through political projects in which new forms of belonging are forged (Cooper 2014: 163). This third layer brings us close to a crucial moment: that of instituting, in which the relations between individuals and things get formalised by means of legal technique. In the case of the Italian movement for the commons, we have seen how this third form of belonging was particularly important. Because activists deployed legal tactics to make the use prevail over the property title and to experiment with direct democracy and self-government, scholars have argued that the movement for *beni comuni* acted as a constituent power, that is, as a collective subject engaged in a bottom-up process of institution-making (Bailey and Mattei 2013). For instance, the occupants of the Valle Theatre resorted to a private legal form, the foundation, as a legal ruse allowing them to formalise their use of the space – to provide this use with temporal continuity. This was a professional use, we may say: the thing reclaimed as commons – the theatre – was one in which a community of occupants, made of artists, actors and cultural workers, could carry out their work. The recourse to the private legal form was thus a way of securing and protecting this direct relationship between the community and the thing – the theatre – also in the future and to provide a long-term legal and political dimension to the occupation.

Identifying this third level of belonging adds a crucial dimension to the previous two: through this stage, property as a bundle of sticks and property as a constitutive relationship can "stand" and endure in space and time. It is in this moment that the political dimension of law, and of private law in particular, is revealed. Private legal rules emerge as the infrastructure of social life and different configurations of rules as implying different distributive effects (Spanò 2022a). As recalled in Chapter 1, the communities that reclaimed cultural spaces as commons in Palermo did not reach the instituent stage in which they could find a legal form for their relationship with the spaces they occupied. However, the reliance on the assembly method for decision-making, together with the production of texts such as manifestos and leaflets, shows that legal-like discourses and practices were produced at the grassroots level, even if the stage of bottom-up legal formalisation was not reached. As a result, in Palermo's cultural commons, property took on a legally pluralist shape, reflecting the existence of a web of relations, not all of which are recognised by the state, and which make it very different from the conventional model of ownership in which a single owner has unlimited control over the thing.

In the next part, the focus shifts to the grassroots practices of urban regeneration carried out in Ballarò, which culminated in the legal formalisation of the re-use market. As I will argue, this experience allows one not only to further explore the third level of belonging, but also to inquire into the complex relationship between things and law, specifically, into how things are constructed through legal technique.

The legal making of things

A materialist and structuralist approach to things

In his essay *La valeur des choses*, published in 2002, Yan Thomas attempted to dismantle one of the main features of modern legal thought: the metaphysics of the subject owner, to whom the total availability of the world belongs. He did so by reversing the perspective and placing himself at the level of things: to downsize the infinite power of the subject owner over the world, Thomas meticulously reconstructed the status of things in Roman law. This quest may be partly reminiscent of Heidegger's work in the 1930s, namely an analysis of things and the conditions that make it possible for a thing to be such a thing. However, this was a metaphysical kind of inquiry, concerned with the being "thing" of the thing (Heidegger 1962; 1973; 1977). Yan Thomas carried out a similar operation, except that he used the legal categories in order to figure out what makes something a thing. The distance between Heidegger and Thomas could hardly be more staggering, but we can imagine how the arguments of philosophical ontology can be tested by the tools of legal technique. If one wants to know how to find things in Rome, this text by Yan Thomas provides some crucial answers. It is a philosophical treatise developed with the tools of the jurist without yielding to metaphysical temptations (Napoli 2022).

The subtitle of Thomas's article is "Roman law outside religion" (*Le droit romain hors la religion*). The French legal historian adopted a materialist and structuralist approach to examine how Roman jurists constructed things. He showed that if we take the perspective of the latter, then we find on their side an element of permanence – of a duration built normatively. Such a construction of things sets aside not only the metaphysical explanations of things but also those of cultural anthropology, in which there is often a subjectivist twist on things. In Thomas's reconstruction, things do not exist in themselves: they are established by legal artifice – normatively made. If there is an ontology of things at work, it is not given but constructed. Things are the objects resulting from a technical construction that occurs through procedure. This, in turn, is a decision qualified by an authority and derived from a legal dispute (Thomas 2002).

Thomas's approach is materialist in that the level of abstraction it reaches is not based on pre-constituted concepts but on the study of legal cases, which in his analysis are the equivalent of fieldwork for the social sciences. Such an approach opens up significant possibilities for dialogue between legal theory and the social sciences: for example, the observation of the mobilisations for the commons becomes a discussion on the transformations of property in contemporary societies. It is this methodological stance that has guided this work, leading to consider the practices first and only then, in this chapter, to return to the legal categories in the light of these.

Thomas's approach is also a structuralist one. Subjects do not exist as a pre-constituted essence but as delocalisations, reflections, secondary effects of a way of thinking like that of Roman law, which gives immediate normative power to the non-human world – to things. We are not talking here about the animal or vegetal world because the critical opposition for Roman jurists was the one between things and persons. The subject does not exist in itself: it emerges in relation to things and does not pre-exist them. Contrary to sociological approaches arguing that norms emerge spontaneously from the level of actors, in Thomas's reconstruction the relations between subjects and things are entirely caught up in a web of institutional relations. The result is not a praise of the sovereign individual over the world but an invitation to find on the side of things an element of permanence and duration that is normatively constructed. This is what can be called a legal ontology of things – an ontology that is not natural but institutionally built. All things, even those that seem most pre-given, such as what we call nature, are produced by the concrete acts of institutions. Even if the latter were to limit themselves to acknowledging the existence of a thing, by this gesture they would have already transformed its supposed naturalness (Thomas 1991).

Thomas developed his theory of institutions on this materialist and structuralist basis. To institute, is first of all, to give things a name, a gesture which has significant consequences for the social order. It is to carry out an operation after which the world will no longer be the same. This operation is simultaneously verbal and practical, as the specific capacity of law is artificial and consists of mixing words and gestures. Law is not only discourse and knowledge; it is also a technique that creates social reality through the invention of forms – this is what instituting means. Instituting does not mean creating from scratch; instead, as Paolo Napoli explains, it means

> to isolate the sequence of frames that make up the shape of reality in such a way that, once the process is complete, it is no longer possible to go back because, in the eyes of the jurist, the recodification of people, things, actions and functions that follows that shaping has produced a concrete abstraction that instantly supplants the empirical datum.
>
> (Napoli 2023: 450)

In the substitution of the empirical datum with concrete abstraction lies the specific capacity of law to impose forms to social reality: the forms are imperfect and infinitely simpler than reality, and they succeed not only in disciplining but also in shaping it. The creation of the institute – a noun disciplining a relationship while qualifying it – is the result of such a process of substitution, which happens through the concrete acts of institutions. It is in this way that, as Yan Thomas insisted, law emerges as the only discourse that produces the world it designates (Thomas 1978). In this abstract and formal quality of the institutes lies the origin of their longevity and adaptability right up to modernity (Spanò 2022b: 152).[1]

The market thing

The process by which social reality is provided with a legal shape is not peaceful. Conflict of different degrees can occurs among the actors concurring in the choice of the norms that will be adopted and in deciding the ways legal forms will be deployed. Let us now return to the Southern Italian commons and look again at the negotiations made to find a legal form for the market in Ballarò. As we have already seen, the market historically emerged in modern Europe as a crucial space of inclusion and exclusion at the same time – a zone of demarcation between civil society and the other individuals not fitting in it (Todeschini 2007). The story of the regularisation of the Ballarò market can be inscribed in this history, as it is a space in which one can observe the delineation between civil society and political society and the mobility of such boundaries. But if we want to add the dimension of legal abstraction to this analysis, then the experience of the Ballarò market has a further layer that has to do not with the civil society/

1 As recalled by Spanò (2022b), in Roman law, the *res incorporales* were legally recognised entities deprived of substance, "things without body", at once concepts and instruments.

political society cleavage but with the legal philosophical and historical meaning of the market space. This dimension is the market as a modern institution and how it gets formalised and re-formalised through legal technique. The vicissitudes of the Ballarò market and those who have reclaimed its use can be read as a moment of renewed formalisation of the market – of a collective negotiation of the norms through which it is governed and accessed. The formalisation of the market space in modern Europe – its construction as a specific cultural, social, economic and legal entity – is a historical process that began in the eighteenth century. Such a construction has a substantial spatial and visual component. As Fernand Braudel wrote, in the Ancien Régime, "le marché, c'est faire surface" (Braudel 1979: 12): the market is designated by public authorities as a specific portion of the urban territory, a space put in place by a set of rules formulated to facilitate the circulation of goods and services. For a long time in European modernity, the market existed in this purely material sense as a physical place for the concentration of social exchange and interdependence. Here, buyers and sellers would occupy the space to ensure their survival. The initial formalisation of the market is thus a very concrete process. It consists of bounding it to a territorial and temporal location – in determining where and when its activities will take place. The moment the market is set up, it can only be localised – and not in any place or time. The market presupposes a space where everyone has to go, identified a priori as the site where transactions occur. Since the market is the place where the needs of different individuals come together, it is also the place to which the political authorities turn their attention to guarantee that exchanges are carried out correctly. A classic and basic historical form of the market is this – an area of public control. The market is always a fraction of the maintenance of public order, if only because there can be frauds happening and thus social instability unfolding, for example, when someone is cheated by another who has sold something that has expired. As Paolo Napoli points out, the functioning of the market as a thing-institution entails a series of divisions: of urban territory, of time, of practices, of goods and money (Napoli 2020: 125).[2]

2 Only later, towards the second half of the eighteenth century, the market started to become something else than a physical space for visible transactions. The market doubled itself, as it were: as an empirical portion of the urban territory, as it had been before, but also as an immaterial place where sellers and buyers are represented abstractly. In analysing this development in the case of Paris, Steven Kaplan spoke of "market place" for the former and of a "market principle" for the latter (Kaplan 1988: 16–18). Paolo Napoli highlights how, in this second moment, the market became an institution of veridiction in Foucault's terms: it lost its link to an essence, to an identifiable space, and became an indicator of social functions that realise the exchange of goods and services. There was, then, a shift from a need for control (market place) to a need for veridiction (market principle). The market was no longer a place of material exchange: individuals entered it as a place of truth (Napoli 2020).

In the case of Ballarò, the process of regularisation of the market that unfolded from the negotiations between activists and the public administration implied a reformalisation of the market in two directions. First, the municipal ordinance adopted in 2019 established opening and closing times and greater inspection and control, which had to be managed through coordination between the police, the municipality and the vendors themselves. This move helped to strengthen the function of the area as a market place – as an empirically measurable perimeter of urban space where buying and selling activities are conducted under public scrutiny. Introducing fixed stalls for vendors is also a way of ensuring the visibility of the activities occurring in the area. These are measures that, together with other rules, such as those included in the Single Regulation of Markets approved in 2016 to improve the conditions of historic markets, lead to a reformalisation of the market along its classical forms. What may appear to be a set of technical and even pedantic administrative rules is, in fact, a way of reinstating this well-established abstraction – the institution of the market as a space of public order. Such a reformalisation aligns with the affirmation of a tourism-based urban economy, which requires greater public control of the areas where value is produced. If there is a physical space where the everyday practices that make Southern Italian cities touristically attractive are tangible and inscribed in urban space, it is the market. Reformalising it means making such practices even more legible and available for consumption. This remains true even though, as we have seen, the touristic transformation in the Italian South implies that value is extracted from something that is not material, namely, the lives and everyday practices of the popular classes. The exploitation of labour takes on biopolitical features: what is being exploited are not the vendors but, more subtly, their livelihoods, of which selling activities are a significant part. Yet, the market provides an important material bulwark and spatial context for such an extraction.

The reformalisation of the market in Ballarò has a further dimension, which has more to do with its symbolic function and social and cultural value than with the physical inscription in urban space. As we have seen, what was legally recognised with the regularisation of the Ballarò market is something that is neither material nor visible: its role as a social safety net and the status of sellers as "vendors by need". These measures point to an even higher level of abstraction than the one described above, in which another mode of transformation of the area is being registered by law: the elevation of the market place to a site of broad cultural and economic significance – a space where attempts are made to counter the spread of urban poverty by promoting cooperation and wealth redistribution. The establishment of the association through which the vendors were provided with legal status contributed to this doubling of the market's meaning: the latter was no longer simply a part of the urban territory subject to public control, but also, through legal abstraction, a social and cultural entity in its own right.

Hacking property: the struggle for the commons in Naples

The long touristification of Naples

It is now worth exploring what other forms of legal abstraction emerged from cities of the Italian South where the commons were reclaimed to oppose the privatisation of urban space and its transformation for touristic fruition. In this part, I turn to Naples as a city in which similar processes to the ones observable in Palermo were at play in the 2010s: a grassroots mobilisation reclaiming resources and spaces left to abandonment and privatisation as commons and a structural transformation of the city's economy in the touristic sense, pursued by local elites of different political views to solve the economic crisis. As I shall explain, the use of law made by activists reclaiming *beni comuni* in the Neapolitan case was different from those observed in Palermo; comparing the two allows to see how different elements of abstraction emerge from the trajectory of the Southern Italian commons and could be synthetised in one consistent legal regime.

The metamorphosis of Naples into a major national and international touristic pole is a historical process that started long before the 2010s. The centre of Naples has the peculiarity of extending both above and underground, and ever since the times of the Grand Tour in the eighteenth century, it has been a tourist destination. Back then, cultivated members of the Northern European bourgeoisie would travel to the Italian peninsula and write reports in orientalist tones describing the Italian South as a liminal territory, a frontier between modernity and backwardness, with Naples epitomising such traits (Mozzillo 1992; Calaresu 2007). It was already mentioned how, after Italian unification in 1861 the Italian *Mezzogiorno* was constructed as the opposite of the progressed and civilised North by public servants and intellectuals. In this phase, in which both foreign and national personalities would denounce the barbaric and backward character of everyday life in the South, Naples was considered the most outstanding example of how the territories previously belonging to the Kingdom of the Two Sicilies needed thorough state intervention to instantiate public order (Moe 2002).

Two events that transformed the centre of Naples in the twentieth century were the Second World War bombings, like in the Palermo case, and the earthquake that hit the city in 1980. On both occasions, the architectural and social fabric of the centre was severely damaged. Many of the abandoned, underused and run-down buildings then became the objects of use of the spaces made by residents that greatly exceeded those foreseen by law, to the point of making the public/private, formal/informal distinction an irrelevant matter.

Then, during the neoliberal phase, things started to change. In 1995, large parts of the city's centre, most of whose historic buildings are publicly owned, were declared a UNESCO World Heritage Site. At the end of the century, public authorities began to promote a broad urban renewal process charged with strong political and symbolic meaning. In the 1990s, during the left-wing administration led by post-Communist mayor Antonio Bassolino, the centre underwent major changes to get rid of the city's image as an outcast among European cities. Against this bad reputation, local elites began building a discourse of valorisation of its rich cultural heritage, which, in their minds, had to become the core of new public policies aimed at rebranding the city's image. The renovated urban space of Naples had to express a different set of standards from those of dirt, decay and crime it was associated with, i.e., the values of decency, civic sense and legality (Dines 2012). This metamorphosis was desired not only by the city's but also the international ruling classes. The commitment to urban reconfiguration was widespread among urban elites of Southern Europe at that time, and it was part of a broader political project: that of affirming a civil society made of a solid middle class concerned with ideas of democratisation, rights and the rule of law forming a unified liberal front in the post-Cold War era (Schneider and Schneider 2001).

While the local elite had already taken the path towards an urban economy with a tourist vocation, some new elements appeared in post-2008 Naples. Since then, tourism emerged as an even more predominant economic and discursive force, triggering dramatic transformations of the city's social fabric in ways that resonate with the concept of austerity urbanism evoked earlier. Studies show how the "airification" of the centre – the fast expansion of Airbnb listings in the historic area – implied a massive relocation of the original inhabitants to the city's outskirts (Cerreta et al. 2020). In 2019, there were more than 7,000 listings for accommodation solutions in Naples on Airbnb and 70 per cent were in the historic centre. These figures did not include the numerous "improvised" Airbnbs that were not officially registered. In the post-2008 crisis phase, public property assets in the centre thus shifted from being a means to secure the right to housing for the popular classes to functioning as a monetised resource to meet increasing amounts of touristic flows and investments. This change was backed by the local government, as proved by a public policy plan called "Destinazione Napoli 2020" adopted by the centre-left wing administration (Caputi and Fava 2019). The document implicitly recognises the accomplished transformation of Naples into a site of what can be called experiential tourism: a specific touristic modality based on the commodification of the residents' everyday life, which becomes available for visitors like any other good. A walk through the alleys of a popular market thus becomes a commodity that can be sold and bought (Bock 2015).

The touristic transformation of Naples has caused controversies and resistance. Among these forms of dissent, an important and organised one is carried out by activists linked to the network SET – Southern Europe against

Touristification. This mobilisation was born in Spain in the late 2010s as a platform to rethink tourism as tied to social and economic justice. A group of protesters connected to SET formed in Naples in 2018, when the city became the most visited urban destination in the Italian South, with 3.8 million tourists (Caramiello et al. 2021). The work of SET in Naples is political – consisting of community organising through regular public assemblies – and speculative, involving researchers and experts who provide a theoretical perspective on the sophisticated mechanisms of value extraction at play in the city. This combination of political practice and theoretical outlook helps linking the materiality of the residents' living conditions with the abstract nature of the financial flows (Rolnik 2019). Ultimately, the aim is to find a shared political grammar for rethinking and subverting the relationship between the two. The issues addressed by SET in Naples, most of which are shared with other tourism-oriented urban economies in Southern Europe, include the increase in precarious work for people employed in the tourism industry, the transformation of commercial activities located in the centre into activities for satisfying the needs of tourists and real estate investors and the erosion of the right to housing caused by public-private real estate speculation.[3]

Reviving civic uses

The rise of the SET group is part of a broader network of mobilisations against the privatisation of spaces and the increase in inequalities that have transformed Naples since the 2008 economic crisis. The Neapolitan movement for the commons has been active since the early 2010s and was successful in obtaining from the public actor the adoption of legal instruments recognising the existence of the urban commons as spaces governed by grassroots communities and for the benefit of the whole population. As early as 2011, the city council, then led by Mayor Luigi de Magistris, included the commons in the municipal charter (*Statuto Comunale*) among the city's fundamental values. A year later, it approved the Municipal Regulation for the Discipline of the Commons (*Regolamento delle consulte per la disciplina dei beni comuni*), and in 2013 another resolution in which the principles for the government of the commons were listed (Comune di Napoli 2011; 2013). Between 2014 and 2015 two further instruments were adopted, which assigned abandoned public and private spaces to community self-government and recognised the capacity of communities to decide over their uses and functions (Comune di Napoli 2014; 2015). In these regulations, the urban commons (*beni comuni urbani*) are defined as

3 *La battaglia del pesone* is the expression used to refer to the fight for the rent (*pesone* is "rent" in the Neapolitan dialect) in which the popular classes have been involved, with the support of various grassroots groups (Caramiello et al. 2021).

"experiences already existing in the territory of the municipality, carried out by groups and/or committees of citizens according to logics of self-government and experimentation of direct management of public spaces, demonstrating the perception of these spaces as places that can be the object of collective fruition for the benefit of the local community" (ibid.). The municipality has thus provided an array of publicly and privately owned spaces with the legal status of commons, owing to their use for social collective needs.

Activists reclaiming the commons in Naples resorted to other legal tactics through which another model of abstraction than the one at work in Palermo can be imagined. Such uses of the law realised the cornerstone of what we may call a non-proprietary ownership: a relation of belonging tying individuals and things in which the most salient aspect is the use that is made of things (Napoli 2015). As anticipated in Chapter 3, this path started in 2012 when a group of precarious art and cultural workers occupied the ex-Asilo Filangieri, a sixteenth-century palace in the centre of Naples. Aligning with practices developing in other cultural spaces across the country, such as the Valle Theatre in Rome and the Garibaldi Theatre in Palermo, the occupants aimed to subtract the space from the use that the owner (the municipality) had decided for it: turning the palace into a site for prestigious cultural events organised by private actors (Capone 2016). The group, following the method of open and public assemblies and with the support of legal experts, eventually resorted to a legal trick to strengthen the claim over the space. This consisted of reviving a residual form of property in the Italian legal system, namely the civic uses (*usi civici*). The activists drafted a regulation offering an extensive interpretation of this institute, which has conventionally been used to guarantee collective access to natural resources, such as timber, for communities living in rural areas. The civic uses were used as the legal form through which to protect the production of non-state forms of welfare, such as self-governed medical cabinets or desks providing assistance to migrants. Activists successfully negotiated with the municipality to adopt their draft at the level of city government and eventually a regulation was issued in 2016 in which the status of commons was recognised for seven occupied spaces on the legal basis provided by the civic uses. The text states that the concerned spaces are commons and that as such they are fully available for communities that decide the rules and forms of government through a collective assembly method (Corbisiero 2019).

From the perspective of legal abstraction, what happened in the case of Naples is of remarkable importance. Civic uses were retrieved from the residual realm in which they were confined as exceptions to the individualistic property regime (Grossi 1977; Marinelli 2013). In the Neapolitan context, they became instruments through which to protect specific uses of spaces and pursue values of solidarity and of a dignified life, not only in the present but also in an intergenerational perspective. Here, a bottom-up constituent power created norms with a potential of subversion and at the same time, inscribed in a perspective of continuity – in which preexisting legal forms adapt to new social practices (Crea 2020).

Private law as the infrastructure of the social

In this chapter, I returned to the experience of the commons in the Italian South to explore which vision of modern legal categories it is possible to develop in light of that experience. The commons of Palermo and Naples contain the elements for elaborating a kind of property law that breaks away from the ordinariness of an individualist relationship of appropriation over things (spaces, resources) to rearticulate itself in a new way – that of the collective, which, through private autonomy, gives itself rules for social and solidaristic uses of things. Two concepts provide the bulwark for this rethinking: belonging as a broader category than property and things as resulting from legal construction. The experience of cultural spaces reclaimed as commons and the grassroots process of urban regeneration of Ballarò flowing into the regularisation of the re-use market lead in this direction. The Neapolitan case allows to see how, alongside the Palermo case, there has been another possible legal signification of the commons in the Italian South, one that has to do with the revival of an ancient legal category to give form to new social uses of things and spaces. The trajectory of the movement for the commons shows how private law functions as the infrastructure of social life and every relationship passes through private legal forms – property being one of them, along with contracts and torts – mediating everything we do (Spanò 2022b). In the end, what appears is the capacity of legal institutes, and of private legal institutes in particular, to function as forms that, although starting from a specific genesis, remain open to be deployed for redistributive political projects.

References

Bailey, Saki and Ugo Mattei. 2013. Social Movements As Constituent Power: The Italian Struggle for The Commons. *Indiana Journal of Global Legal Studies* 20(2): 965–1013.

Bock, Kerstin. 2015. The Changing Nature of City Tourism and Its Possible Implications for the Future of Cities. *European Journal of Futures Research* 3(1): 1–8.

Bollier, David. 2020. Commoning as a Transformative Social Paradigm. In *The New Systems Reader*, London: Routledge.

Braudel, Fernand. 1979. *Civilisation matérielle, économie et capitalisme, XVe-XVIIIe siècle, vol. II – Les jeux de l'échange.* Paris: A. Colin.

Bresnihan, Patrick and Michael Byrne. 2015. Escape into the City: Everyday Practices of Commoning and the Production of Urban Space in Dublin. *Antipode* 47(1): 36–54.

Butler, Judith. 2009. Critique, Dissent, Disciplinarity. *Critical Inquiry* 35 (4): 773–795.

Calaresu, Melissa. 2007. From the Street to Stereotype: Urban Space, Travel and the Picturesque in Late Eighteenth-Century Naples. *Italian Studies* 62 (2): 189–203.

Capone, Nicola. 2016. Del diritto d'uso civico e collettivo dei beni destinati al godimento dei diritti fondamentali. *Politica del diritto* 4(XLVIII): 597–636.

Caputi, Alessandra and Anna Fava. 2019. Napoli in vendita. Tra turismo e privatizzazioni. *Critica Urbana* 7: 11–16.

Caramiello, Marzia, Paolina de Notaris, Giulia Renzi and Geremia Trinchese. 2020. Napoli è indomabile e quindi non succederà? *Scomodo*. www.leggiscomodo.org/napoli-turistificazione.

Cerreta, Maria, Fernanda Della Mura and Giuliano Poli. 2020. Assessing the Interstitial Rent: The Effects of Touristification on the Historic Center of Naples (Italy). In *Computational Science and Its Applications – ICCSA 2020*, Lecture Notes in Computer Science, Osvaldo Gervasi et al. (Eds). Cham: Springer International Publishing, pp. 952–967.

Cooper, Davina. 2014. *Everyday Utopias: The Conceptual Life of Promising Spaces*. Durham, NC: Duke University Press.

Corbisiero, Fabio. 2019. I beni comuni come antidoto alla turistificazione dei centri storici? Il caso di Santa Fede Liberata a Napoli eds. Musarò Pierluigi and Piga Bruni Emanuela. *Scritture migranti* (13): 154–176.

Crea, Camilla. 2020. "Spigolando" Tra biens communaux, usi civici e beni comuni urbani. *Politica del diritto* 3: 448–464.

Dines, Nick. 2012. *Tuff City. Urban Change and Contested Space in Central Naples*. New York and Oxford: Berghahn Books.

di Robilant, Anna. 2013. Property: A Bundle of Sticks or a Tree? *Vanderbilt Law Review* 66(3): 869–932.

Grossi, Paolo. 1977. *Un altro modo di possedere. L'emersione di forme alternative di proprietà alla coscienza giuridica postunitaria*. Milan: Giuffrè.

Heidegger, Martin. 1962. *Die Frage nach dem Ding: Zu Kants Lehre von den transzendentalen Grundsätzen*. Tübingen: De Gruyter.

Heidegger, Martin. 1973. *Kant Und Das Problem Der Metaphysik*. Frankfurt am Main: Klostermann.

Heidegger, Martin. 1977. *Phänomenologische Interpretation von Kants Kritik Der Reinen Vernunft*. Frankfurt am Main: Klostermann.

Linebaugh, Peter. 2008. *The Magna Carta Manifesto: Liberties and Commons for All*. Berkeley, CA: University of California Press.

Marinelli, Fabrizio. 2013. *Gli usi civici*. Milan: Giuffrè.

Moe, Nelson. 2002. *The View from Vesuvius: Italian Culture and the Southern Question*. Berkeley, CA: University of California Press.

Mozzillo, Atanasio. 1992. *La frontiera del Grand Tour: Viaggi e viaggiatori Nel Mezzogiorno borbonico*. Naples: Edizioni Scientifiche Italiane.

Napoli, Paolo. 2015. Il Comune: Un'appartenenza non proprietaria. *Alfabeta2*. www.alfabeta2.it/2015/04/25/il-comune-unappartenenza-non-proprietaria.

Napoli, Paolo. 2020. Instituting Revisited: For a Materialistic Conception of the Institution. In *What's Legit? Critiques of Law and Strategies of Rights*. Zurich: Diaphanes, pp. 111–127.

Napoli, Paolo. 2022. L'inappropriable. Lecture at the EHESS (7 December 2022).

Napoli, Paolo. 2023. Variazioni sull'adagio: La natura può fare a meno dell'uomo. *Filosofia politica* (3): 447–464.

Rolnik, Raquel. 2019. *Urban Warfare. Housing under the Empire of Finance*. Translated by Felipe Hirschhorn. London: Verso.
Schneider, Jane and Peter Schneider. 2001. Civil Society Versus Organized Crime: Local and Global Perspectives. *Critique of Anthropology* 21(4): 427–446.
Spanò, Michele. 2022a. *Fare il molteplice: Il diritto privato alla prova del comune*. Turin: Rosenberg & Sellier.
Spanò, Michele. 2022b. Cose senza corpo. Forma e materia degli istituti giuridici. In *Sulla soglia delle forme. Genealogia, estetica e politica della materia*, Anna Montebugnoli (Ed.). Milan: Meltemi, pp. 149–163.
Thomas, Yan. 1978. Le droit entre les mots et les choses. Rhétorique et jurisprudence à Rome. *Archives de philosophie du droit* 23: 93–114.
Thomas, Yan. 1991. Imago Naturae. Note sur l'institutionnalité de la nature à Rome. *Publications de l'École Française de Rome* 147 (1): 201–227.
Thomas, Yan. 2002. La valeur des choses. Le droit romain hors la religion. *Annales. Histoire, Sciences Sociales* 57(6): 1431–1462.
Todeschini, Giacomo. 2007. *Visibilmente crudeli. Malviventi, persone sospette e gente qualunque dal Medioevo all'età moderna*. Bologna: Il Mulino.
van der Walt, Andries Johannes. 2009. *Property in the Margins*. Oxford and Portland, OR: Hart Publishing.
Watson, Alan. 1998. *The Digest of Justinian, Vol. 4*. Philadelphia, PA: University of Pennsylvania Press.

Legal sources

Comune di Napoli. 2011. 'Individuazione e approvazione di alcuni principi in tema di concezione dell'acqua come bene comune e indirizzo per la trasformazione dell'ARIN S.p.A. in soggetto di diritto pubblico' (Deliberazione di Giunta Comunale n. 740 del 16/6/2011).
Comune di Napoli. 2013. 'Approvazione dei principi per il governo e la gestione dei beni comuni della città di Napoli' (Deliberazione di Giunta Comunale n. 17 del 18/1/2013).
Comune di Napoli. 2014. 'Proposta al Consiglio. Indirizzi per l'individuazione e la gestione di beni del patrimonio immobiliare del Comune di Napoli, inutilizzati o parzialmente utilizzati, percepiti dalla comunità come "beni comuni" e suscettibili di fruizione collettiva' (Deliberazione di Giunta Comunale n. 238 del 24/4/2014).
Comune di Napoli. 2015. 'Indirizzi per l'individuazione e la gestione di beni del patrimonio immobiliare del Comune di Napoli, inutilizzati o parzialmente utilizzati, percepiti dalla comunità come "beni comuni" e suscettibili di fruizione collettiva' (Deliberazione di Consiglio Comunale n. 7 del 9/3/2015).

Conclusion

In *The Prison Notebooks*, Antonio Gramsci uses the expression “the mystery of Naples” to refer to what seems like an anomaly in the city’s socioeconomic structure. The inhabitants are industrious and intensely engaged in economic activities, and yet they are not considered productive in conventional terms because their occupations are not aimed at satisfying the needs of the ruling classes. Gramsci links this phenomenon with the class composition of the biggest city in the Italian *Mezzogiorno* and its peculiar historical origins. In Naples, a relatively small class of owners is surrounded by a plethora of artisans, hawkers, middleman, intermediaries and layabouts constantly engaged in a diverse array of activities which break down the trade flows and service deliveries into very small parts. This *sui generis* kind of productiveness, Gramsci argues, is a major feature not only of Naples, but also of other Southern Italian cities, where economic life thrives in a context of absence or scarce presence of industries, and the economic sector considered as productive – the one in which goods are created and accumulated – is of a relatively small size (Gramsci 1977).

In the cities of the Italian South, value is extracted precisely from the non-productive realm making up the mystery of Naples – from the life of the individuals who keep it alive. Many recent episodes provide examples of this process. In July 2017, the luxury fashion house Dolce & Gabbana organised a five-day show in Piazza Pretoria, in the heart of Palermo’s historic centre. A few metres from the Quattro Canti (the centre of the city which divides it into the four *mandamenti*), the square is the site of Palazzo delle Aquile, the seat of the municipality, and a monumental sixteenth-century fountain in which human figures and fantastic creatures are depicted. The square is commonly called “Piazza della Vergogna” (square of shame) by the residents, in reference to the naked sculptures but also to a local power associated in the past to corruption and scandals. The sumptuous event, authorised by the city council and organised by the two stylists – one of whom was born in the nearby village of Polizzi Generosa – was meant as an ode to Palermo. A stylised version of the Sicilian popular imaginary – made of baroque architectural elements, icons of saints, carts

DOI: 10.4324/9781003335320-6

and *cassate* – provided the symbolic material on which the clothes and the show were realised. Part of the event took place in the nearby Palazzo Gangi, whose salons are famous for having been the location of Luchino Visconti's *Il Gattopardo*. Another catwalk was staged on the hill overlooking the city in front of the Cathedral of Monreale, which was recently declared a World Heritage Site by UNESCO. These shows involved a ban on the access to public space for anyone not taking part in the catwalks, even at night. Despite the enthusiasm of the local elites, the catwalk was greeted with scepticism by those who saw it as "a form of occupation" of the urban space, a "show for the rich that exploits Palermo's beauty by precluding it to the public".[1] These criticisms did not account for an essential element which was revealed in this episode. The closure of public space to host a private fashion event, in which the works on display are inspired by Sicilian culture and iconography, is tantamount to perpetuating the primitive accumulation of this territory's capital, without which the catwalk would not have been possible in the first place. In the Italian South, the touristic transformation is not only a form of oppression of the popular classes; it is also, importantly, a process of value extraction. While the exploitation and manipulation of local culture and traditions to make economic profit is not a new phenomenon in modern Italy, what is unprecedented is reducing the urban poor's form of life to a commodity.[2]

Similar fashion shows took place in other Southern Italian cities over the past years, including Naples and several towns in Puglia. When in 2023 a Japanese billionaire booked whole sections of Palermo's centre to host his birthday party, the Politeama Theatre was rearranged as a dinner location for 1,400 guests and the opera house, the Teatro Massimo, was reserved for a private concert.[3] The prophecy of Oscar Farinetti, the entrepreneur and founder of Eataly who once declared that the Italian South should be turned into "an immense Sharm-el-Sheikh", thus seems to be coming true (Conelli 2022). Activists are aware of this political project and oppose it on a symbolic, discursive and political plan. With Palermo's touristic metamorphosis now blatant, a large banner appeared in the streets of the city in July 2024, during the celebration of Santa Rosalia: "touristification is the new plague – where has my house ended up?". With this slogan, the local group tied to the SET

1 'Dolce & Gabbana sfila a Palermo tra lusso, entusiasmo e polemiche': www.artribune.com/progettazione/moda/2017/07/dolcegabbana-sfila-a-palermo-tra-lusso-entusiasmo-e-polemiche.

2 Lombardi Satriani's *Folklore e profitto* explained already in the 1970s how the marketing of peasant and popular cultures works and how, in the Italian case, its historical roots are in the fascist cultural project of re-ruralisation of the country (Lombardi Satriani 2021).

3 'Sicily, where billionaires get back to basics – by booking an entire city': www.theguardian.com/commentisfree/2023/nov/05/sicily-where-billionaires-get-back-to-basics-by-booking-an-entire-city?CMP=share_btn_url.

network launched a collective assembly to discuss new modes of resistance against the spread of mass tourism.

In this book, I explained how the mobilisation for the commons in the Italian South interacted with the reconfiguration of urban economies in a touristic sense in the aftermath of the 2008 financial crisis. I highlighted how the struggle among different actors on how to reshape urban space amidst this transformation implied the co-existence and clash of different political and legal concepts of the commons. Some of these diverse, at times competing ideas of *beni comuni* are rooted in the recent history of the Italian South while others are anchored in the core values of neoliberal capitalism. Different articulations of the commons correspond to the making of different subjectivities, which are also legally crafted – produced as legal subjects. In contemporary cities, then, the commons can be deployed to realise a disciplinary ordering of urban space tied to new forms of value extraction. But they can also envisage an alternative relationship between individuals and things – one of belonging, through which the absolute and exclusive idea of property predominating in modern legal thought is dismissed and the collective can be instituted. This ambivalence in the political and legal use of the commons is not surprising if we keep in mind what political life is like in a context of transition as was the case of Italian society in the 2010s. As E.P. Thompson wrote, the "stress" of transition implies that "resistance to change and assent to change arise from the whole culture", and this includes power and property relations (Thompson 1967: 80).

The scholarship on the commons is very vast and includes contributions from disciplines such as legal theory, legal geography, critical legal studies, urban sociology, cultural studies and socio-legal studies. In this book, I decided to address only a few of these scholarly fields, hoping to provide new conceptual and methodological tools to study a subject that has been thoroughly analysed from multiple perspectives and yet, perhaps precisely for this reason, risks losing its analytical potential after its extensive introduction into social and legal studies. This work does not aim to be a comprehensive book on the theories and practices of the commons, but an attempt to engage in a conversation with different groups of readers interested in delving into issues of socio-legal relevance through the prism of the commons. In each chapter, I addressed one of these audiences and proposed the following main points:

1 That the mobilisations for the commons do not take place in a void but depend on specific social and cultural histories and are restrained by the values orienting public action in each scenario. In the case of the Italian South, the local trajectory of the anti-mafia movement as well as the emergence of the discursive orders of legality and participation in the after-crisis conjuncture, both at the national and international level, played a crucial role in providing such coordinates. This is what I tried to show in Chapter 1, in which I discussed a range of practices conducted under the label of

commons in Palermo during the 2010s. I chose to limit the observation to three groups of experiences, differentiated by the underpinning methods and values, the relation with the public actor and the rights that were being claimed, although some aspects did overlap. I looked at the occupations of cultural spaces, the anti-mafia urban regeneration of public spaces and the reappropriation of a market space by a collective of activists and vendors. The former two sets of practices fit within a perimeter of possibilities that is discursively determined by ideas of legality and participation. I explored both as emblematic of the neoliberal transformation of Italian society in the 2010s, traced their links with the complex history of the anti-mafia movement and focused on the subjectivity of the active citizen that they produce – a moral subject committed to producing welfare through volunteer work. I presented the legal instruments through which these values became tools of government and explored how the related subjectivity emerged as a subject, namely a set of administrative regulations adopted in hundreds of Italian cities in the 2010s conceptualising the commons as a tool to discipline and regulate urban space. The focus then shifted to the practices that lie outside of the realm of public action thus defined. I deployed the notion of political society, borrowed from postcolonial studies, to refer to a population that accesses the economy and reclaims rights outside of formal structures. In this realm, radical ideas of legality and participation are pursued by activists reclaiming spaces and are mobilised in the negotiation with public authorities to adopt tools in which the property interests of the marginalised residents are protected.

2 That the extended recourse to the label of commons to legitimise diverse social demands reveals how this concept is available to serve a broad set of political projects, ranging from emancipatory ones linked to power and wealth redistribution to others in which the urban space is disciplined and sanitised. This is the main argument proposed in Chapter 2, addressing readers interested in critical theory and legal sociology. I explained that if the commons function as an umbrella-claim, this is also due to part of existing scholarship romanticising the groups reclaiming them, a literature which posits such actors as autonomous communities in an unrealistic neither-public-nor-private-field. The practices of the movement in the Italian South reveal the entanglement of individuals and groups reclaiming the commons with both the state and the market and their constant involvement in the negotiation of the structures, including legal ones, in which the meaning of the commons is contested and established. I believe that future research should focus on the racial and gendered dimensions of the communities reclaiming the commons – on how hierarchies of race and gender embedded in private property are reproduced or challenged by the commons as a legal concept. Two further points are developed in the chapter. The first one is that elements of the mobilisations for the commons were absorbed in the national and local policy framework, paving the way for a touristic

reconfiguration of urban economies. The second one is that the everyday life of the political society living in Southern Italian cities became the backbone for new processes of value extraction. This aspect is essential for the contemporary renewal of Italy's Southern Question, the structural imbalance between the North and the South of the country that is both symbolically and socioeconomically produced and that shows how the national project and capitalist transformation have proceeded hand in hand.

3 That despite an increasing resort to legal tactics by social movements in crisis-ridden contexts over the last decades, scepticism persists among activists who mistrust law as an emancipatory tool and tend to identify it with its repressive function or the violent end of power. This is the argument advanced in Chapter 3, in which I engage in a conversation with scholars from socio-legal studies and critical legal studies. I traced how equating law with its punitive side is theoretically justified even by certain strands in critical theory and based on a flattened reading of parts of Marx and Foucault's thinking. I put this conception to the test of the experience of the Southern Italian commons to argue that another idea of law emerges from such practices: one in which the negotiation for determining how to govern urban space prominently takes place in the legal field, where what is at stake is the content of public and private legal rules and any alleged line separating "the legal" and "the political" is hard to draw. I then suggested a non-exhaustive array of arrangements that are available here and now, in existing legal systems, that can be mobilised to secure the property interests of the marginalised and to enact property as an emancipatory political project. I focused on three sets of instruments, namely community land trusts, public law regulations and civic uses, as helpful tools for protecting the everyday lives of the popular classes from commodification. I propose that reconceiving property from the city's margins means finding, especially in private law, a repertoire of tricks through which the predominant conception of property is contested, power and wealth redistribution is realised and the interests of political society are prioritised. I pointed to the ongoing theoretical debate and case law advancements on the representation of non-human entities as the most a promising realm in which legal tools for instituting the collective are developed.

4 That it is possible to interpret the movement for the commons as a process in which a core form of modern law, property, has been deeply contested and reshaped from the grassroots. If we look at the story of the movement for the Southern Italian commons in terms of its impact on property forms, what we extrapolate are signs of the gradual dissolution of the absolute, individualistic and exclusive idea of property that is predominant in modern legal thought. Belonging – *pertinere* in Roman law – is a category that can be retrieved through a genealogical excavation of modern legal forms which qualifies a relation between individuals and things that goes beyond mere appropriation.

Such is the meaning, in terms of legal abstraction, of the emergence of use as a paramount form for the relation between individuals and things practiced by movements in post-crisis Southern Italian cities. I also presented a theoretical complement of property as belonging, namely a notion of things as normatively built – as produced and reproduced through the concrete acts of institutions, as the case of the open-air market regularisation exemplifies – and of the subject as emerging as a reflection of the object, an effect of the relation binding them. These are the two arguments advanced in Chapter 4, in which my interlocutors are in the field of legal theory and legal history, and my aim is to integrate the focus on the philosophical and sociological dimensions of the Southern Italian commons with a reflection on the theoretical legal implications of their appearance. I argue that the experience of the commons ultimately gives us important hints for thinking about institutions in a materialist sense, as an ever-changing outcome of praxis, and away from deterministic temptations. It also shows how the activity of private subjects is the foundation of a law intended not as an array of bans and prohibitions but as a set of constantly perfectible descriptions of material and symbolic relations (Napoli 2020).

The choice of writing chapters that differ in their intended audience, although situating themselves in the same, wide field of law and social sciences, will hopefully not result in a fragmentation of the topic – the broad spectrum of political and legal practices that have been labelled as commons in recent years – or in a weakening of the descriptive force of this concept. Rather, my purpose is to bring together diverse readers in an investigation of the commons as an elusive object for socio-legal studies from which to interrogate the ways in which property, citizenship and labour are changing in contemporary societies. In this exploration, as always, the questions are more important than the answers.

References

Brown, Wendy. 2015. *Undoing the Demos: Neoliberalism's Stealth Revolution*. New York: Zone Books.

Conelli, Carmine. 2022. *Il rovescio della nazione. La costruzione coloniale dell'idea di Mezzogiorno*. Naples: Tamu Edizioni.

Gramsci, Antonio. 1977. *Quaderni del carcere*. Turin: Einaudi.

Lombardi Satriani, Luigi M. 2021. *Folklore e profitto. Tecniche di distruzione di una cultura*. Palermo: Edizioni Museo Pasqualino.

Napoli, Paolo. 2020. 'Instituting Revisited: For a Materialistic Conception of the Institution'. In *What's Legit? Critiques of Law and Strategies of Rights*, LizaMattutat, RobertoNigro, NadineSchiel and HeikoStubenrauch (Eds), pp. 111–127. Zurich: Diaphanes.

Thompson, E. P. 1967. Time, Work-Discipline, and Industrial Capitalism. *Past & Present*, (38): 56–97.

Index

For Product Safety Concerns and Information please contact our EU
representative GPSR@taylorandfrancis.com
Taylor & Francis Verlag GmbH, Kaufingerstraße 24, 80331 München, Germany

www.ingramcontent.com/pod-product-compliance
Lightning Source LLC
LaVergne TN
LVHW021247011026
849160LV00010BA/970

9781032371030